C000273207

THE CROCHET WORKBOOK

THE CROCHET WORKBOOK

Sylvia Cosh and James Walters

B. T. Batsford Ltd, London

Title page photograph by Rex Moreton

Photography and drawings by Sylvia Cosh and James Walters

First published 1989

ISBN 0 7134 5915 8

Typeset by Deltatype, Ellesmere Port
and printed in Hong Kong
for the publishers
B. T. Batsford Ltd
4 Fitzhardinge Street
London W1H 0AH

Contents

Acknowledgement

We would like to thank everyone who has attended our crochet workshops for all the things they have taught us – in particular Delsey Neville for her practical approach to working in the round (method 2). In this book we have included work by Mavis Bell (76b), Iris Smith (83h) and members of our 1988 Knitting Craft Group Summer Workshop Weeks (10 and 63). Thanks also to Mary Lamb Becker for advice on US crochet terminology; to Lydia Ault, Brenda Donelly and Pat Rhodes for their hard work over the years making things for us; to Amanda Cosh (big hugs) for modelling; and to our families, friends and colleagues for their constant advice, practical help and warm support, especially Jan Messent, Pauline Turner (The Crochet Design Centre), and Geoff and Colinette Sansbury (Colinette Yarns), Stephen Sheard (Rowan Yarns) and Alec Dalglish (The Knitting Craft Group of the British Hand Knitting Association). To find out more about Mind Maps (chapter 4), look for books by Tony Buzan.

Introduction

This book is intended for people of all ages (and both sexes), for existing crocheters who are looking for a new dimension to their work, and also for people who may never have picked up a crochet hook before. We assume that you will want to experience crochet from the inside and to experiment with it spontaneously and freely from the beginning. (Beginners may not be aware that, in many ways, this is easier, as well as more rewarding, than following conventional pattern instructions or working in the conventional way!)

The word 'free' means many things to us: it refers mainly to freedom from the limitations of the conventional approach and, beyond that, to escape from the restrictions we all unknowingly impose upon ourselves through blind habit, which programmes our thoughts and responses so that they become automatic and so involuntary. 'Free' means being aware, being able to generate new options and to make fresh choices whenever we need. This may sometimes include seeing when a conventional approach will get us to where we want to go, and choosing to go for it!

We do not have the space to show the absolute basics here (these can be easily picked up elsewhere, and it is up to you to do so), but we do give some important guidance for beginners. This is, in any case, not just a manual on crochet techniques, nor is it a pattern book. It is more a personal trip, showing how involvement with crochet can go beyond hooks, stitches and even yarns, and how none of us has to be restricted to reproducing a standard commodity or matching a norm. We hope you will be interested to try our approach and will be entertained by it. Once you have dabbled, however, we also hope you will press on with the main quest for your own personal creativity and individual style.

Lefthanders

Apologies to lefthanders! Since righthanders are in the majority, our drawings have been prepared to suit them. Please be assured, however, that crochet itself has no stupid bias of this kind and does not demand that you do anything in a right-handed way. In most of the important places, we have inserted a miniature mirror-image version of the main illustration, which we hope will help; otherwise, if you can arrange to view the main drawings in a mirror you will see what you should be doing.

US terminology

One area in which the 'special relationship' between Great Britain and North America seems to have fallen apart is that of crochet terminology! Whereas the actual mechanics of crochet are the same for all of us, the names of the stitches are not. Or rather, just to be confusing, the names for the stitches *are* the same, but seem to have slipped one place in the list and so refer to *different* stitches (see p. 92 for a comparative list of terms and abbreviations). It might have been easier if an entirely different set of names had evolved on either side of the Atlantic. This is not really much of a problem, so long as you are aware of the situation. In any case, we have put both expressions in the text whenever possible with the US term in square brackets [ ].

Have fun!

1a, b, c *Modern crochet rejoices in colour and texture, whether it be quietly beautiful, or thoroughly lively and exuberant*

1
What is crochet?

Traditional and modern crochet

As crochet is such a simple, almost obvious, craft, it is tempting to believe that its origins are as old as mankind. There is very little real evidence, however, that it goes back more than a few hundred years, when it seems to have been the work of nuns. In nineteenth-century Europe there was a vogue for lace, and crochet was found to be a suitable technique for quick and cheap copying of many of the established styles of needle and pillow lace. A cottage industry was started to satisfy demand. Eventually the fashions changed, and by the time of the First World War crochet had all but disappeared. Before then, particularly in Ireland, some extremely vital, original and amazing work had been created – much of which was characteristically freeform lace (69).

Nowadays, even when, from time to time, the fashion for fine lace returns, few people are prepared to sit and make it by hand – even in crochet. More often we go for thicker yarns to make crochet 'knitwear'. Crochet is now one of the most instant and affordable ways of making distinctive and personal garments.

Crochet attracts some people because it gives them something to do with their hands. What starts as a hobby, however, can sometimes take over, become totally absorbing and even develop into a passion. Dedicated enthusiasts may undertake immensely time-consuming fine or large-scale work to cover tables, beds, walls or even windows (2).

As it requires no loom, wheel, or other heavy equipment, and is one of those crafts which works very well as patchwork, crochet is highly portable and convenient for people on the move. It is also wonderful for co-operative group projects in schools and other communities.

Some people treat crochet as an art, a medium of personal creativity and self-expression. They use it for yarn paintings, hangings and soft sculptures, but not for anything practical, except perhaps 'wearable art' (3). It is extraordinary that a craft offering such a rich range of possibilities is not more popular. When, however, the colourful butterfly finally breaks out of its antique lace cocoon, it dazzles with the splendour of its secret transformation (1a). More people are being drawn to take crochet up – now what will it become in *their* hands?

2 *The design of this 'window hanging' was suggested by the shape, subtle patterns and natural colours of a moth's closed wings. It was a challenge to fit this almost 5m (over 15 feet) high triangular window – particularly as the two 'halves' were far from symmetrical!*

3 We find that the only way to obtain a full range of matching tones through a wide variety of yarns of different qualities and textures is to dye them ourselves

The hook

You can crochet with your fingers or, more usually, with a special hook. In the past, hooks have been made by hand out of wood or bone; nowadays they are professionally made in steel or plastic to a precise set of sizes (these are different in the USA and Europe – see p. 93).

Most serious enthusiasts will, sooner or later, need a good range of different sized hooks to match the different thicknesses of the yarns they like to work with. The most important thing about your hooks is that they should work well in your hands, and you should feel comfortable with them. Notice (4) that the tip of a good hook has a subtle profile and a beautiful shape (the mass-produced market leaders are generally excellent); do not waste time with simply or crudely fashioned hooks, however cheap they are, because they are frustrating to work with.

The yarn

Traditionally, crochet is associated with smooth, fine, cotton yarns in white, cream, beige and écru. The recent revolution in yarn design and return of practical interest in handspinning have, however, made available a wonderful profusion of colour and texture, to which modern crochet enthusiasts are drawn just as eagerly as the knitters and weavers for whom the yarns are primarily intended. Yarns of all kinds (6) are your raw material; if you love them and take great pleasure in holding them and working with them, you are in grave danger of becoming a crochetaholic!

If you are a beginner, start with a smooth yarn, which makes things easier. Just as soon as you can handle the basic movements, go for exotic and exciting yarns. These are the real joy of crochet today.

Your yarn hoard is your crochet palette. For rich and creative work, it is essential to build up an enormous collection of different colours and textures – even a simple project, with a limited range of colours, can require several tens of different samples. Eventually, you will be able to draw the nucleus of the yarns you are going to need for each new project from your stock. In the meantime, beg or buy even just a ball or a hank every time you happen to see something interesting (or irresistible!) and keep it sorted according to its colour family.

4 *A hook with a subtle and beautiful shape works much better than a crudely made one*

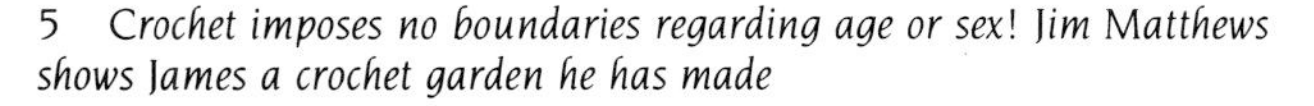

5 *Crochet imposes no boundaries regarding age or sex! Jim Matthews shows James a crochet garden he has made*

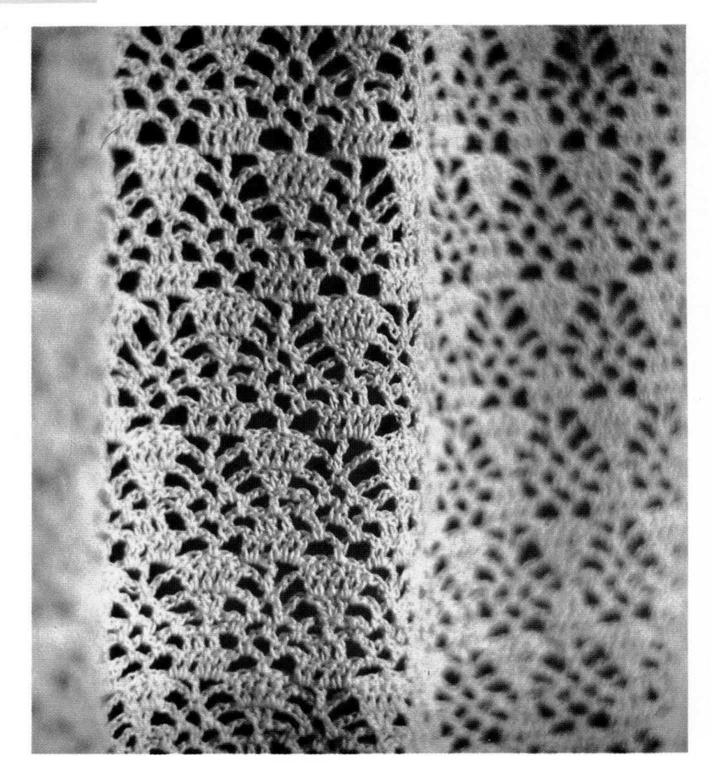

7 *Conventional crochet openwork*

8 *Ever-decreasing circles*

Yarn into fabric

Crochet fabric is made by continually drawing loops through previous loops made in a continuous thread. As with knitting (but unlike weaving, tatting and lacemaking) the structure involves no knots – until you fasten off, it all unravels when you pull back on the yarn. The simplest stitch consists of a single loop and turns the single strand of yarn into what looks like a chain link. Simple lace fabrics are made from arches of chains, which are anchored to each other periodically to form a trellis. Solid fabrics (that is, those with no deliberate holes) can also be made, as in knitting, by making stitches row upon row, into stitches in the row below.

It is usual to work to and fro in straight rows to produce flat squares and rectangles (You can change the shape of the fabric as you go by increasing and/or decreasing the number of stitches in the rows). Since each stitch locks the previous one into place, it is not necessary to hold an entire row of stitches on a second pin as in knitting. This means that there is no problem with 'dropped' stitches. It also means that rows can easily be made to curve or zigzag, and even to go round and round in rings or spirals to make flat circles (8), hexagons, pentagons, squares and triangles.

Whether worked 'to and fro' or 'in-the-round', the height/depth of a stitch – almost always much greater than in knitting – can be varied from row to row, or even during a row, to make waves or add texture.

Texture is one of the main fascinations of crochet. There are plenty of simple techniques – all part of the basic procedures – for creating lumps, bumps, knobbles, bobbles and ridges (9). The fabric is in any case generally thicker, firmer and less elastic than knitting. It usually has a textured look rather than the smoothness of, say, knitted stocking stitch.

Crochet is quick to make, lies flat and is easy to measure whilst the work is still in progress. It also provides great flexibility of approach. If you like, you can design and plan a project on a regular grid which corresponds to straight and even rows of stitches running from side to side or from top to bottom of your fabric, exactly as in knitting and weaving. You then use arithmetic to work out from a sample swatch how many stitches and rows you need to make each pattern piece come out in the size and shape you want. You can also then work out decorative patterns and designs on graph paper.

On the other hand, you can forget about any regular structure and work to fill an outline of the shape you want.

9 *Lumps, bumps, bobbles and knobbles*

Without necessarily having any particular preconceived idea of how you are going to proceed, you can work intuitively and experimentally, putting bits here and there, adding more when, where and how it seems suitable. Think of the individual stitches as building blocks – like bricks, but more flexible: the taller the bricks get, the more loops they have in them, but the width stays the same. If you change to a thicker or thinner yarn and/or hook, the bricks become bigger or smaller all round.

This way of working (10), which is what we are most concerned with here, is rather like doodling with coloured and textured pens, except that now you can often change your mind over and over again, right up to the last moment when you are satisfied with the arrangement and choose to join everything into the finished piece.

There is in crochet an enormous range of potential to suit people with completely different tastes, interests, approaches, personalities and talents. What, we wonder, does it have to offer you?

10 *Crochet 'doodling'. These pieces were made in less than an hour by a handful of students playing 'Crochet consequences' at a Knitting Craft Group summer workshop*

2
Crochet techniques

Arm yourself with a book on the basics, and let us guide you through it to where you want to be!

The terminology

Remember that, despite the battery of complicated-looking names, there is only one basic stitch-making procedure in crochet. The terms chain, slip stitch, single crochet, double crochet, treble, double treble, triple treble (. . . and even quadruple and quintuple treble!) do not represent essentially different stitches, but just the standard process chopped up into different lengths.

If you want to be able to follow traditional pattern instructions, or the drift of books such as this one, it is necessary to know the names of the standard stitches and/or to recognise their international symbols. (You can, of course, do your own creative work without ever following any standard procedures or knowing any of the names for anything!)

The skills

Although crochet skills are simple, as with all physical procedures, at the very beginning they may *seem* more tricky than they really are and it may take a little time before they become second nature. It will not matter at all how long it takes to pick them up and to become comfortable with a crochet hook – there are certainly no prizes offered for speed.

Choose hook and yarn

Begin with a smooth, pale-coloured double knitting |US: sport weight| yarn with size ISR 4.00/5.00mm |US: 5/7 or F/G| hook, or a chunky |US: bulky| yarn with size ISR 6.00/6.50mm |US: 9/10 or I/J| hook.

Holding hook, yarn and work

The process of crochet is like writing: everyone does it differently. We each hold the pen in our own way, and our writing is unique. Our ambition is not to make it standard, uniform or anonymous! There is nothing 'right' or 'wrong' about any particular way of holding yarn or hook – plenty of quite different ones are used very effectively in different parts of the world. If you are already a hand knitter, for example, it may feel peculiar to control the supply yarn with the left hand and much more natural to do so with the right. So feel free to do it that way!

The trick with controlling the supply thread is to clasp it just strongly enough to make it easy to catch in the hook and draw through, but not so much that the chains become tight. Unless you are using very fine, slippery yarn, you will probably not need to wrap it around the little finger. As you practise, you will develop your own methods, which will quickly become second nature.

Slip knot

Note that, unlike hand knitting, this initial loop on the hook does not count as a stitch until you make something of it.

11 *Chains*

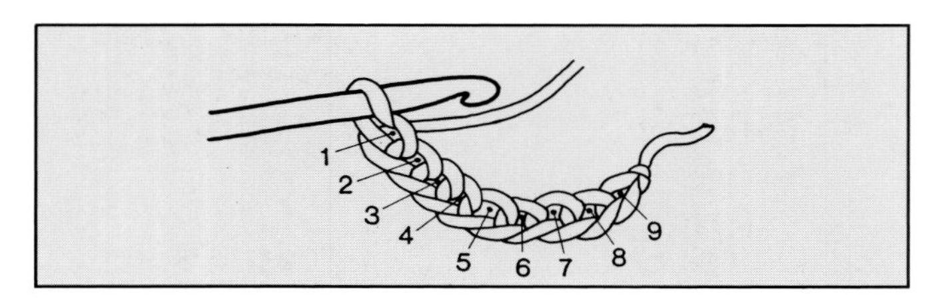

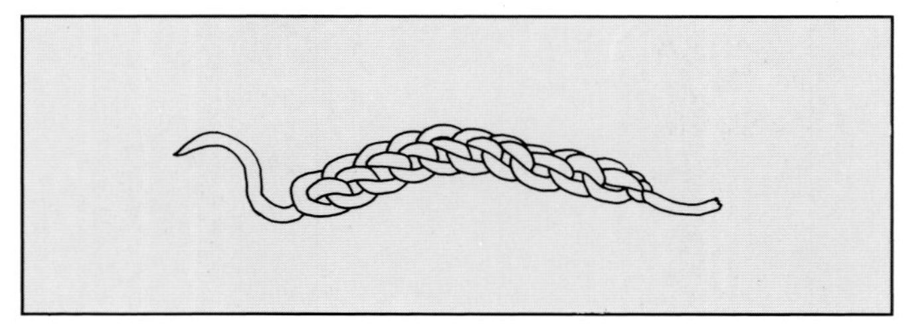

Chain stitch (ch)

For practice, make lots of chains – perhaps for bangles, necklaces, wriggly wigs, hangings or whatever – until you can make them in a relaxed way, but at the same time swiftly and evenly. Learn to see which is the front and which the back of a length of chains, so that you can tell if they are twisted.

In the beginning, never try to make more than two or three chains without shifting the left hand grip right back up to the hook.

Counting

When counting how many chains you have made (11), *do not* count the loop on the hook (the working loop).

Basic stitchmaking

Most drawings of the individual stitches show them being worked into their own base chain, which is the usual way to begin. It is much more sensible, however, for beginners to learn their stitches and practise initially by working their first row into the edge of some other piece of fabric, say, felt, leather, interfacing, or any stable, yet flexible, fabric you can get a hook through (12). If necessary, make a few holes approximately 1cm |3/8in| apart.

It is much easier to learn the stitches in this way, because there is no problem in deciding where the hook should be inserted and no difficulty in doing so. You can also distinguish clearly between the threads of the stitch you are making and the fabric into which you are working, which avoids confusion. Later it will matter exactly where

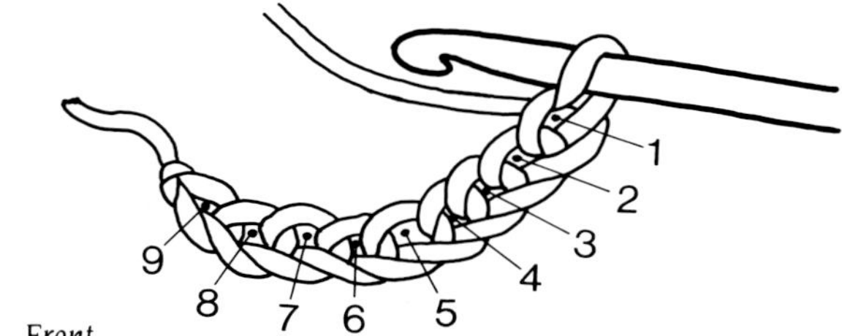

a *Front*

b *Back*

and how the hook is inserted into your fabric, but, for the moment, separate that in your mind from the procedure of stitchmaking.

Begin by making a slip knot and a slip stitch into the first hole. Then make the same number of chains you would normally make for turning (depending upon the size of stitch you are working) to count as the first stitch. If the holes seem to be too far apart, occasionally work twice into one hole.

Most books take you through the stitches in a logical order – from the smallest with the fewest steps to the more complex. Unfortunately they do not point out that the very smallest – slip stitch and double crochet [US: single crochet] – can give you more problems than longer ones, as they make it more difficult to see what you are doing from the second row onwards. It is therefore well worthwhile leaving them alone and coming back to them when you have some familiarity with the various movements.

Longer basic stitches

Longer stitches (12) are all simple extensions of treble [US: double crochet] and have the same four stages. The more wrappings you do at stage 1, the more work there is to do at stage 4 and the taller the stitch becomes. In conventional crochet the tallest stitches you will normally find in solid work are those with two wrappings, but those with three, four or even five sometimes crop up in lace work. In free-form textured crochet and in your own experimental work, there is no theoretical limit!

At the same time, there are chances to make different 'half' stitch variations (like htr [US: hdc]) by drawing through more than two loops during Stage 4. This is not done in conventional crochet, but there is no reason why *you* cannot do it, if you want to.

12 *The four stages of basic stitchmaking*

1 *Stage 1: wrap the yarn around the hook (or not!) – the more times, the longer the stitch will be*
Stage 2: insert the hook into the next stitch (or opening)
Stage 3: wrap the yarn around the hook again and pull a new loop through the fabric only

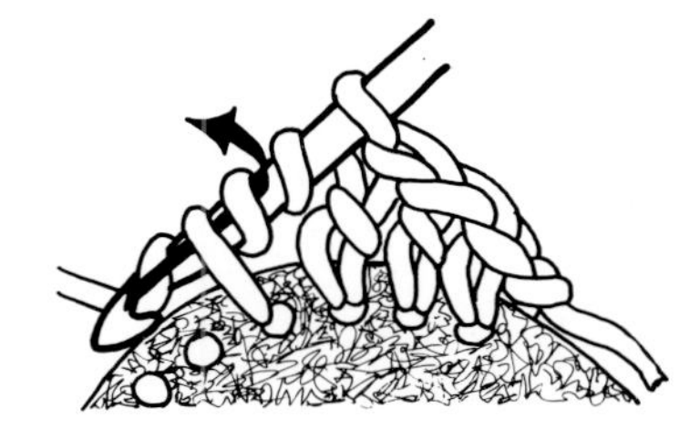

2 *Stage 4: yrh and draw through two loops only . . .*

3 *. . . and do that again . . .*

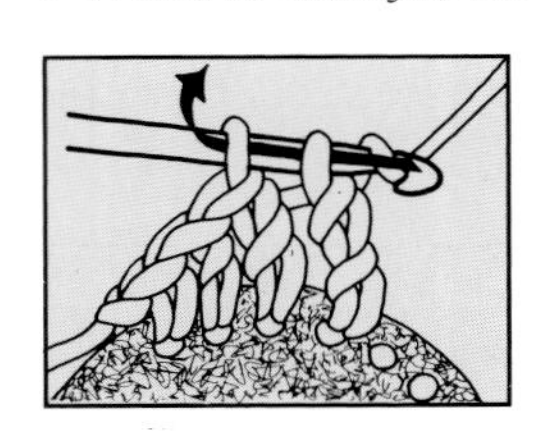

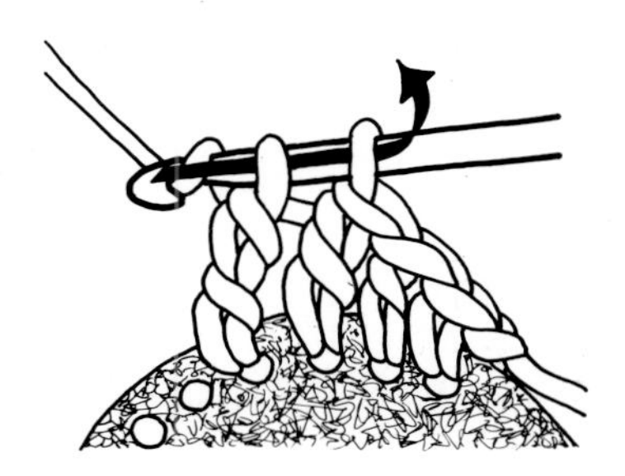

4 *. . . and again . . .*

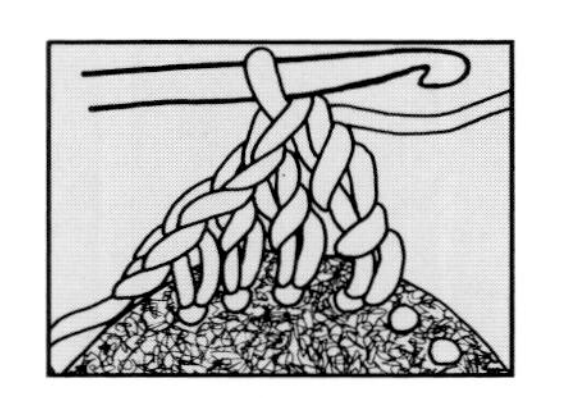

5 *. . . as necessary, until there is only one loop left on the hook. The stitch is now complete! Stitches shown (in order of working): dc, htr, tr, dtr [US: sc, hdc, dc, tr]*

13 *Stitch profiles*

Stitch *(abbreviation)* [US *equivalent*]	**Symbol**	**Stage 1** *Yrh*	**Stage 2** *Insert Hook*	**Stage 3** *Yrh, draw through fabric only*	**Stage 4** *Yrh, draw through 2 loops as many times as necessary until 1 loop remains*	***Extra chs in base ch**	***Work into base ch** *(counting from hook)*	***No. of chs for turning ch**	**Abbr**
Chain (ch)	○	No	No	**draw through loop on hook**	No				*ch*
Slip stitch (ss)	●	No	Yes	**draw through fabric and loop on hook**	No	1	2nd	0	*ss*
Double crochet (dc) [US: *single crochet (sc)*]	+	No	Yes	Yes	Yes (×1)	1 (2)#	3rd	1	*dc* [*sc*]
Half treble (htr) [US: *half double (hdc)*]	T	Yes (×1)	Yes	Yes	**draw through all 3 loops**	1 (2)#	3rd	2	*htr* [*hdc*]
Treble (tr) [US: *double crochet (dc)*]	(treble symbol)	Yes (×1)	Yes	Yes	Yes (×2)	2 (3)#	4th	3	*tr* [*dc*]
Double treble (dtr) [US: *treble (tr)*]	(double treble symbol)	Yes(×2)	Yes	Yes	Yes (×3)	3 (4)#	5th	4	*dtr* [*tr*]
Triple treble (ttr) [US: *double treble (dtr)*]	(triple treble symbol)	Yes (×3)	Yes	Yes	Yes (×4)	4 (5)#	6th	5	*ttr* [*dtr*]

**The details given here are for reference. Treat them as guidelines to be varied in some circumstances.*

#The figures in brackets apply when the turning chain does ***not*** *count as a stitch.*

Working to and fro

Base chain

Usually you need to make more than the number of stitches you want in the row, because extra are needed (13), according to the height of the stitches in the row, to give them room to stand upright.

Turning chain

At the beginning of every row from the second row onwards you usually have to work extra chains – collectively called the 'turning' chain (tch) – for the same reason.

First row

When working the first row of stitches into the base chain, it is important to keep the chain untwisted with the front facing you. By all means insert the hook under two threads of each chain or under one. Experiment to find which is preferable and then be consistent, to avoid confusing yourself!

Turning

By all means turn the work at the ends of the rows in the *opposite* direction to the one indicated, if you prefer (experiment to find out). But be consistent!

Second row onwards

Notice the standard way to insert the hook (from the front and under the top two loops which sit on top of each stitch and look like a chain from above) and stick to it for the moment. There are, of course, variations for specific effects, which you will discover and want to experiment with later.

There is a tricky little thing about crochet which looks at first glance as though it was designed solely to make difficulties for beginners and give them a hard time. It also trips up people who have been doing crochet for years – particularly if they never had it explained to them when they began! That thing concerns the turning chain. Sometimes, for all kinds of reasons which will emerge over time, you will want to *count it as a stitch* (we generally do so) and sometimes you will not! If you do not know, or do not care, or would not know the difference, your ability to control the number of stitches you have from row to row will fly right out of your own hands straight into those of evil-minded demons! Your stitches will tend to dwindle disconcertingly or fluctuate desperately, no matter how loudly you curse or humbly you pray! The goods news is: if you follow through the basic stitchmaking exercise with only four stitches in the row, you can teach yourself both treatments for all time, and need never look back.

Sometimes, in verbal pattern instructions, the designer does not make it clear what you are expected to do in this respect, and you must seize the initiative. One of the immense advantages of the international stitch diagram system is that this ambiguity simply does not exist.

Turning-chain-as-stitch

We suggest you make yourself familiar first with this way of working (14a). Begin by working in treble [US: double crochet], because it is more difficult to see what you are doing with smaller stitches. Do not be tempted to have more than four stitches (counting the turning chain) in the row. You need to become confident at handling the beginnings and ends of the rows as soon as possible and you need to be really sure how many stitches you have at all times. Remember:

1. You *do* count the turning chain as the first stitch at the beginning of every row.
2. To continue working 'straight' (without increasing or decreasing overall) you therefore do *not* work a real stitch into the top of the first stitch (i.e. the last stitch worked at the end of the previous row) . . .
3. . . . but at the end of the row you *do* work a real stitch into the top of the turning chain.

Simple turning chain (*not* counting as a stitch)

We suggest (14b) the best way to be quite sure what you are doing is to repeat the whole first exercise (with just four stitches to begin with) in the same way as for turning-chain-as-stitch, but with these new rules:

1. You do *not* count the turning chain as a stitch at the beginning of the row.
2. To continue working 'straight' you therefore *do* work a real stitch into the top of the first stitch (i.e. the last stitch worked at the end of the previous row) . . .
3. . . . but you do *not* work into the top of the turning chain at the end of the row.

Now you can see how you could get into a muddle, if you mixed these treatments in the same piece of work without knowing what was happening! Whichever treatment you are using, always check at the end of each row that you still have exactly four stitches in the row and that they are all in the right places. It does not matter what your work looks like at this stage (fabric with as few as four stitches in the row never looks very neat or straight-edged) and you should simply concentrate on getting the mechanics right.

As soon as you can work confidently in treble [US: double crochet], then half treble [US: half double], then double crochet [US: single crochet] for several rows each, you can go on to 'increase' then 'decrease' again, working several rows with each stitch (19a and 19b).

Double and treble chains [US: single crochet and double crochet chains]

As soon as you are ready, make yourself familiar with double (15) and treble chains (16). The procedure is very useful, not just for making thicker cords and ties, but for alternative base chains, for increasing and for freeform crochet.

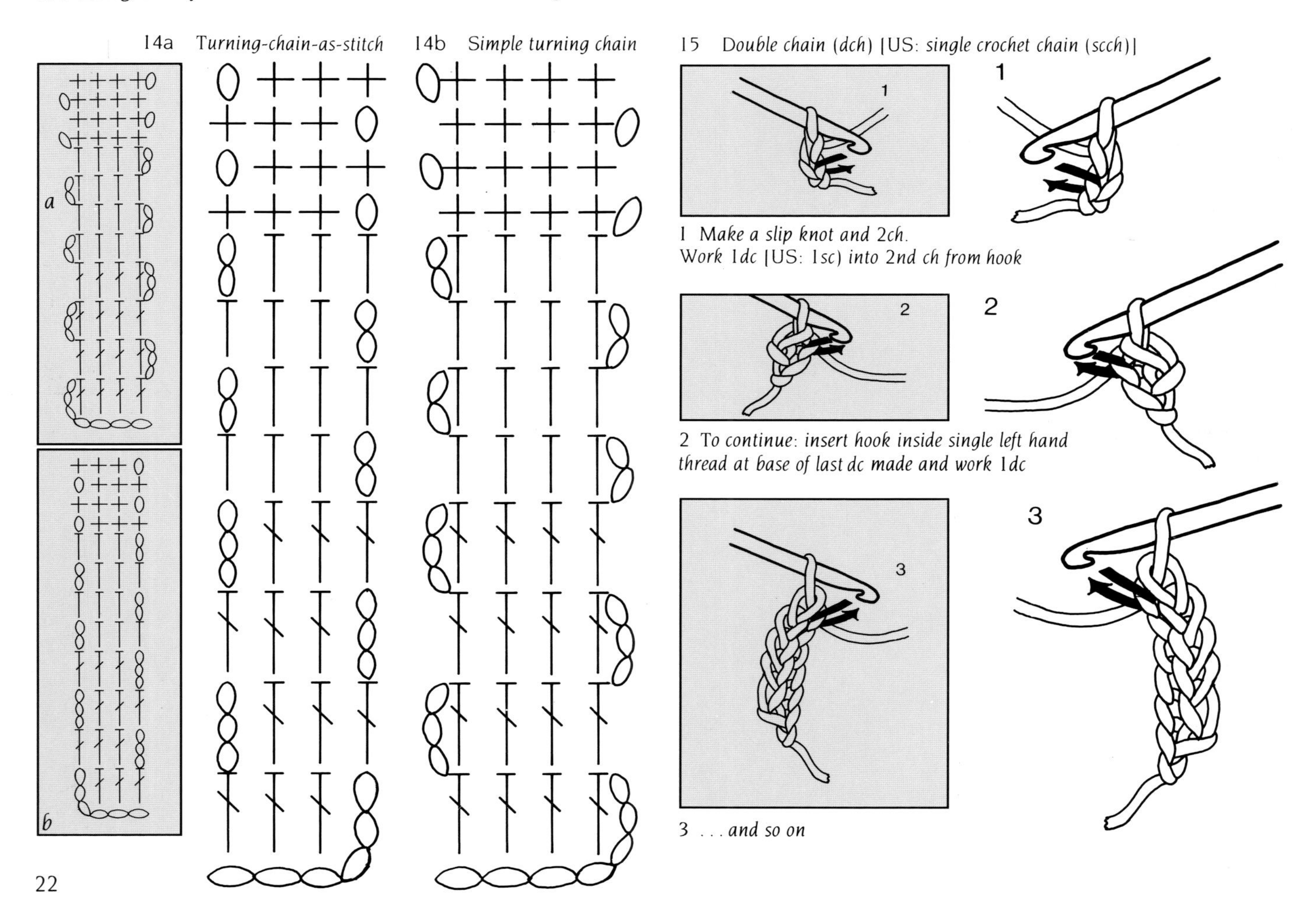

14a *Turning-chain-as-stitch* 14b *Simple turning chain*

15 *Double chain (dch)* [US: *single crochet chain (scch)*]

1 *Make a slip knot and 2ch. Work 1dc* [US: *1sc*] *into 2nd ch from hook*

2 *To continue: insert hook inside single left hand thread at base of last dc made and work 1dc*

3 . . . *and so on*

Shaping

In order to control edge shaping properly, you must first be able to work 'straight', which means understanding and being completely happy about the two treatments of the turning chain (see above) and only mixing them if you mean to.

Increasing

Increasing is usually a matter of working more than one stitch into the same place. An increase of several stitches at the beginning of a row involves making extra chains, which are treated like a new base chain.

Step increase at row end – method 1

The orthodox way of adding several stitches at the end of a row (17a) is to stop working temporarily, make a new base chain with another ball of yarn and join this to the end of the row with a slip stitch. Then you can resume working and continue along the extra chains.

16 *Treble chain (trch)* [US: *double crochet chain (dcch)*]

1 *Make a slip knot and 3ch. Work 1tr* [US: *1dc*] *into 3rd ch from hook*

2 *To continue: yrh and work 1tr inserting hook inside single left hand thread at base of last tr made*

3 *. . . and so on*

Step increase at row end – method 2

Another method, which is often more convenient (17b), is simply to continue working after the end of the row by inserting the hook into the side of the base of the previous stitch, as in double and treble chains (see above). You must remember, however, to make the extra stitches one step (one preliminary wrapping) taller than the previous ones.

17 *Step increase at row end*

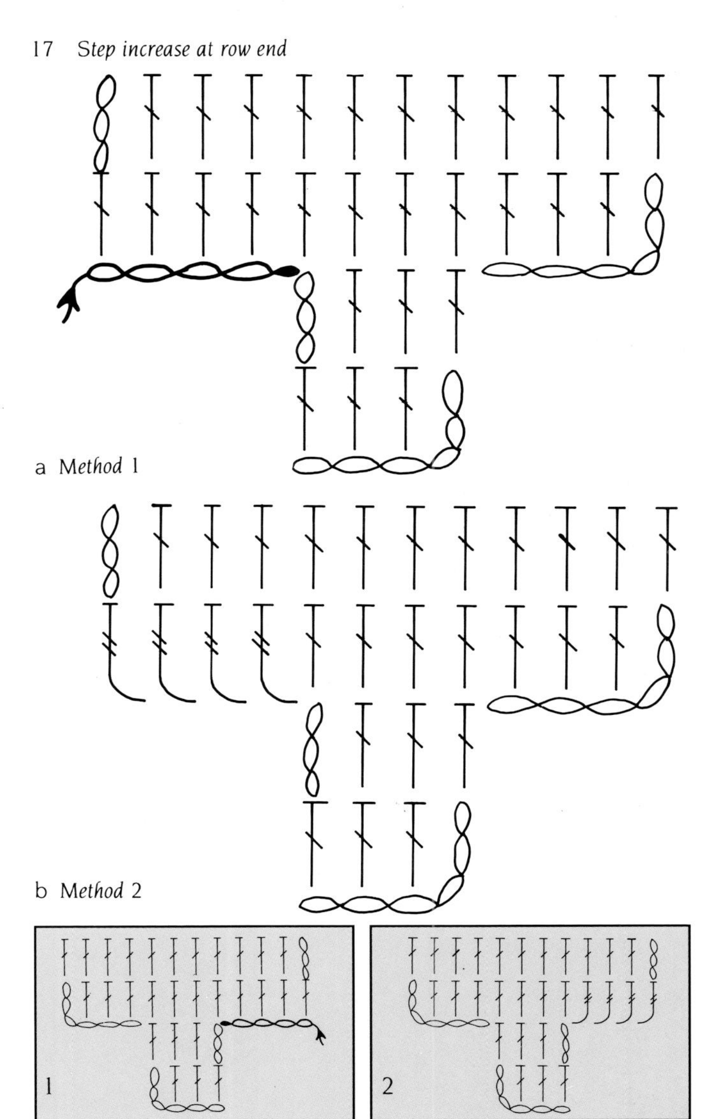

a *Method 1*

b *Method 2*

Step decreasing

At the beginning of a row, decreasing several stitches at once involves either fastening off and rejoining the yarn, or working in slip stitch over the stitches to be eliminated.

Crude decreasing of one or two stitches at a time can be achieved by missing stitches, but this is unsatisfactory, except in the case of the very short stitches, unless you find steps and unscheduled gaps attractive. A smoother method is to join stitches together into one at the top – called 'making a cluster'.

18 *Cluster*

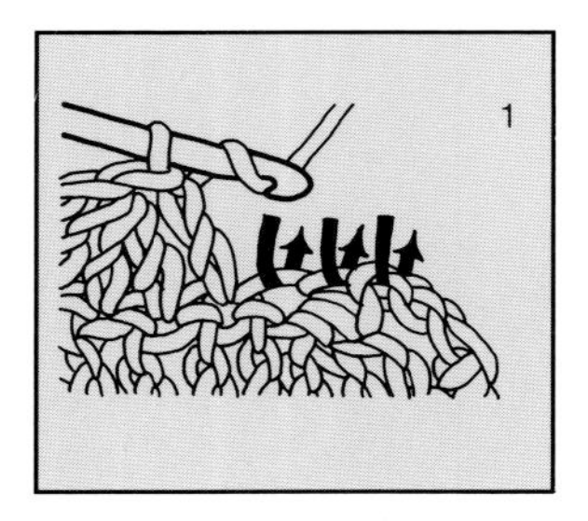

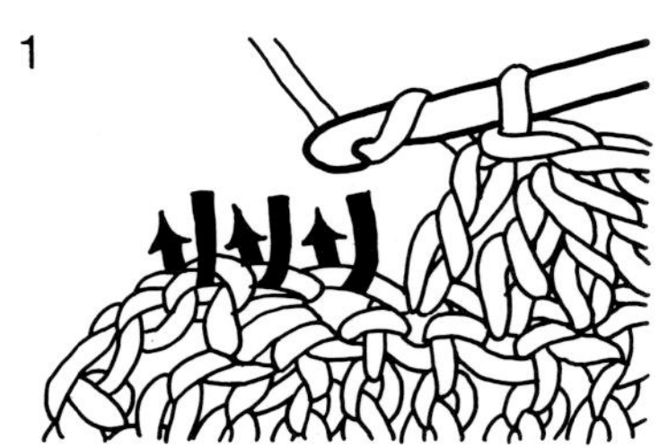

1 *Work each stitch, which is to be part of the cluster, as normal as far as its last step*

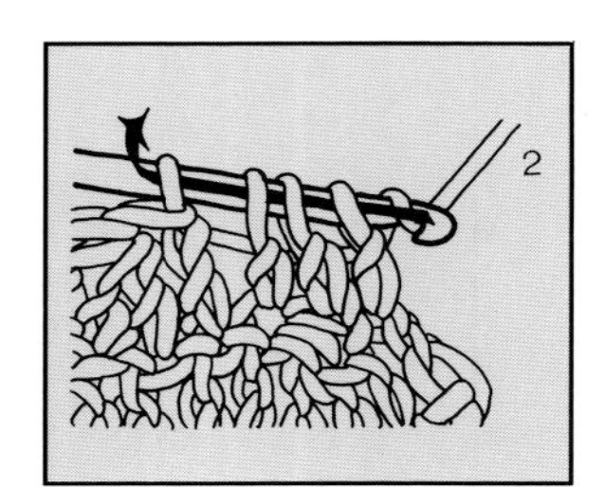

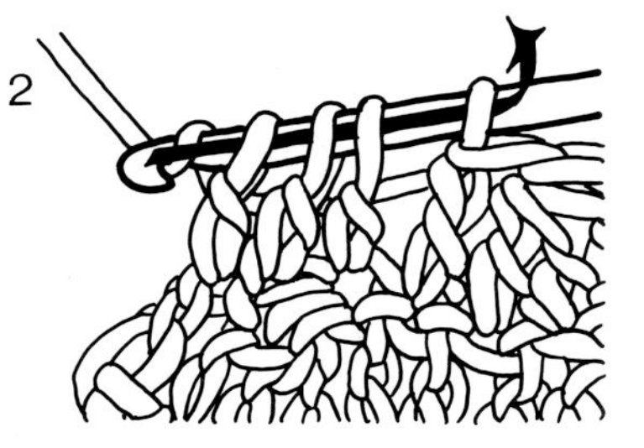

2 *To complete the cluster: yrh and draw through all loops on hook*

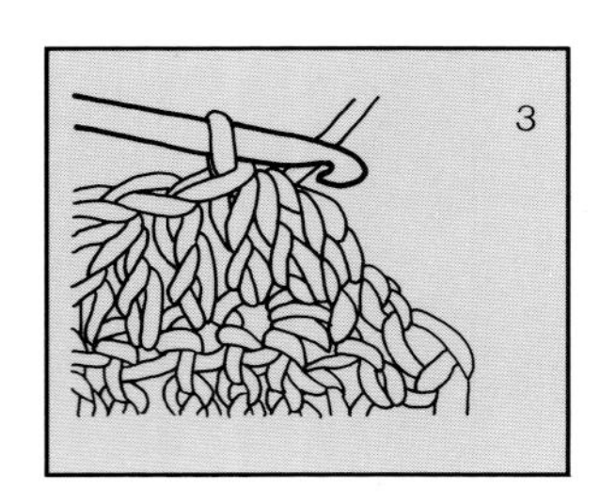

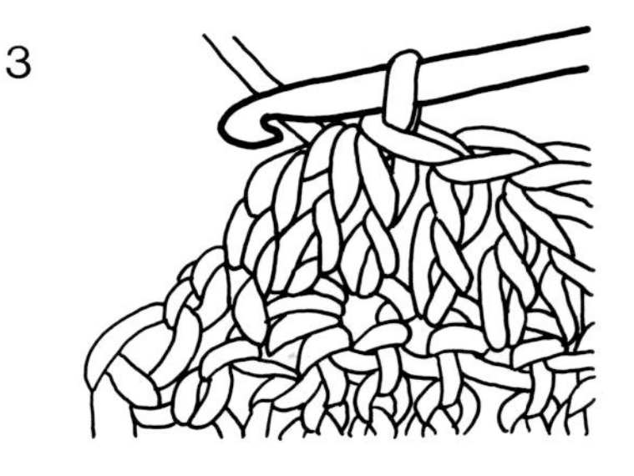

3 *Joining 3 stitches together (as shown here) decreases by 2*

A cluster

To make a cluster (18) of two or more stitches, work each individual stitch quite normally up to, but not including, its last step (the last 'yrh'). At this moment there should be only one loop left on the hook for each stitch in the cluster, plus the working loop which was there to start with. Notice also that the yarn goes direct from the top of each stitch to the top of the next without going around the hook in between (if it does, you have not gone far enough with the later stitch!). Now complete the cluster and join all the

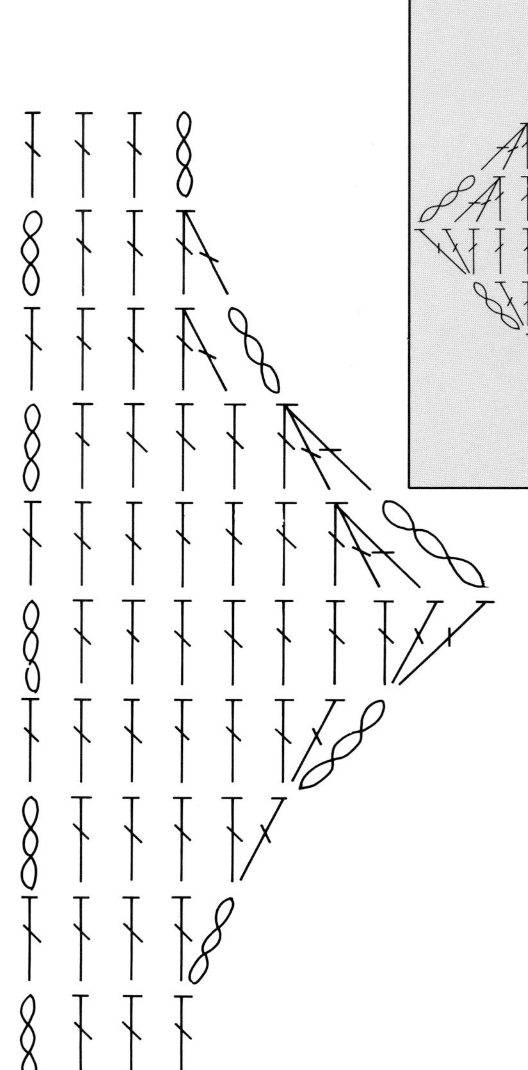

19a *Increasing/decreasing – turning-chain-as-stitch*

stitches into one by working that last step for all of them at once as follows: yrh, draw new working loop through all remaining loops on hook.

The shorter the stitches involved, the fewer it is possible to join into a cluster. Otherwise, there is no real restriction on what assortment of stitches may be worked.

It pays to make yourself familiar with the way that shaping works using both 'turning-chain-as-stitch' and 'simple turning chain' treatments (19).

19b *Increasing/decreasing – simple turning chain*

Curves and chevrons

Owing to the height of crochet stitches the process of increasing and decreasing can be used to change the direction of the rows, rather than the shape of the fabric (20). If you keep the same net number of stitches in each row, there will be no 'shaping' to the fabric – the edges will remain straight and parallel to each other.

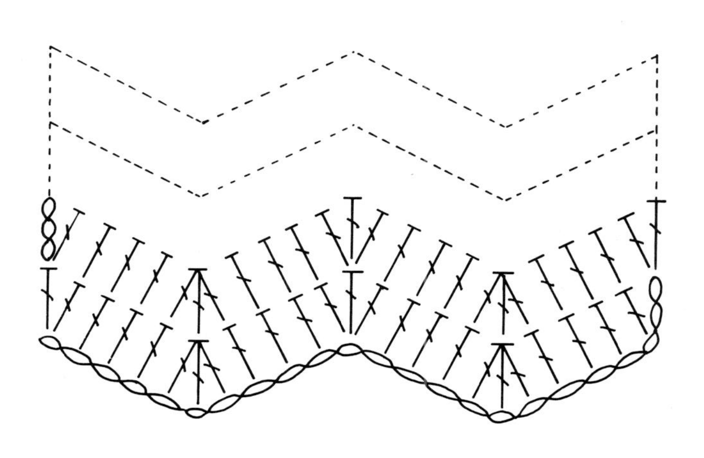

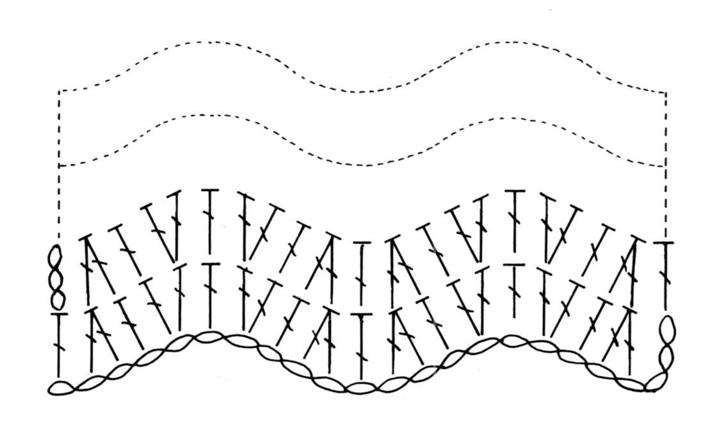

20 *Curves and chevrons*

Working 'in-the-round'

In crochet the expression 'in-the-round' includes a number of things and it is wise to find out what they all are right away (21).

Tube

'In-the-round' may simply mean joining the edges of your fabric together so that you have a continuous tube instead of a flat shape with edges.

Flat round

It may also mean building up the fabric by working round and round a central point or ring.

Tubes may be worked 'straight' [US: even] or shaped (by increasing or decreasing), but flat rounds must involve increasing as you work away from the centre to keep the work flat. Flat rounds need not necessarily be literally circular – traditionally they are often hexagonal, square or triangular.

Both tubes and flat round shapes may be made in either spiral formation or closed rounds.

Spiral

This means you work round and round in the same direction, the same side of the fabric is always facing you and the continuous row ends only when you decide to stop. To begin or end this process without a 'step', you may need to work a few stitches of gradually increasing or decreasing height.

Spiral formation may be the easiest to work – people do

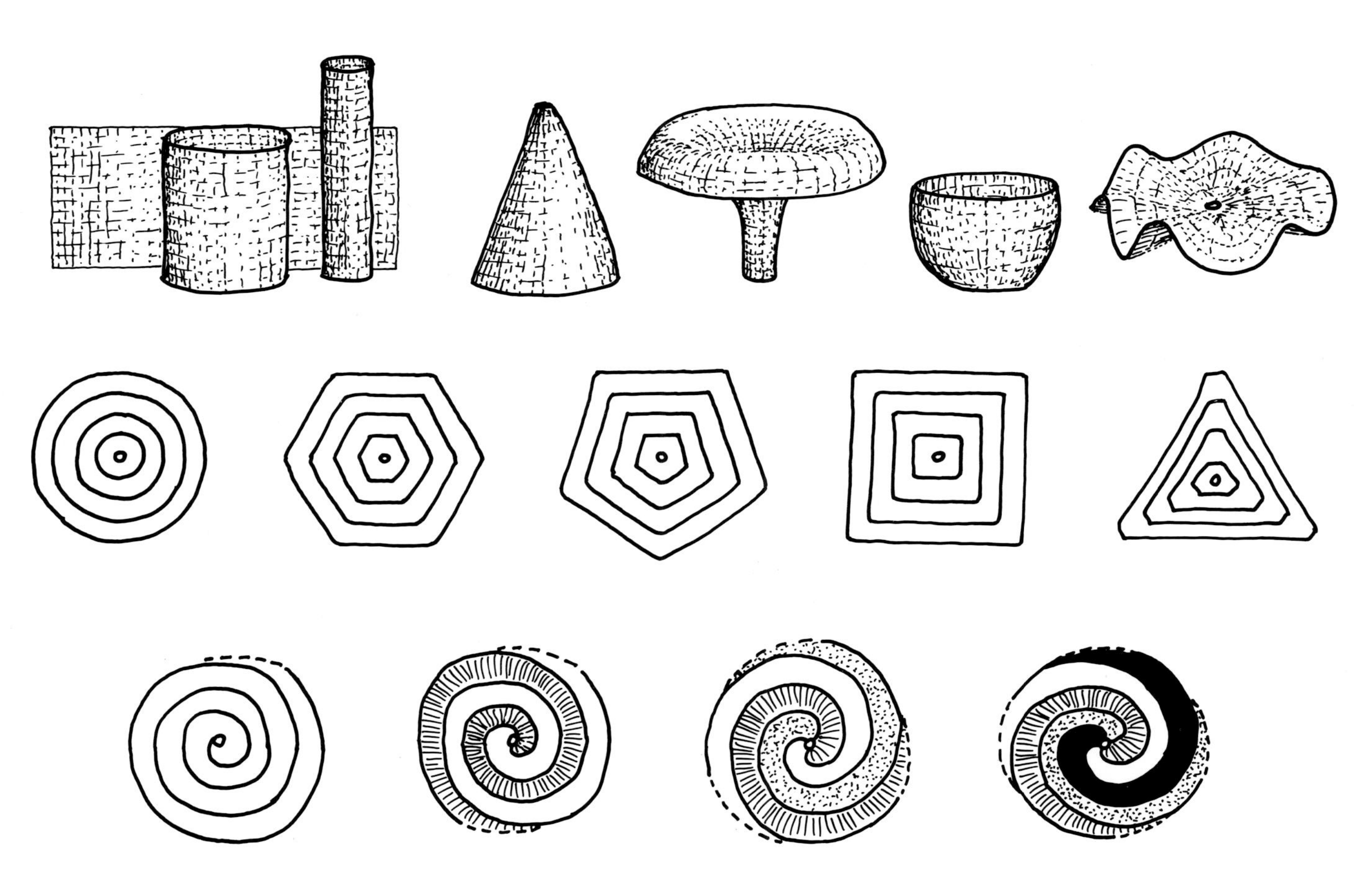

21 *'In-the-round' shapes*

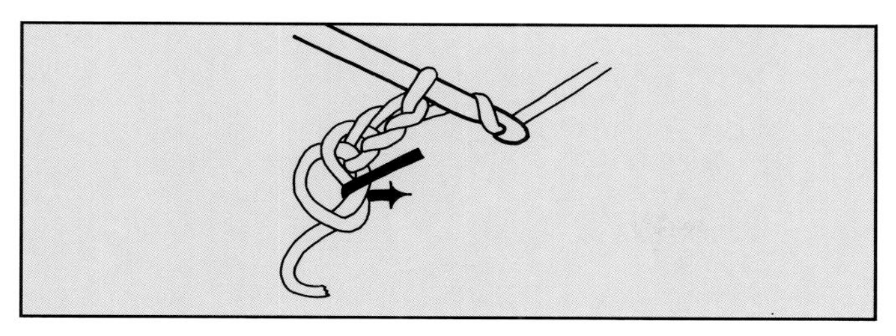

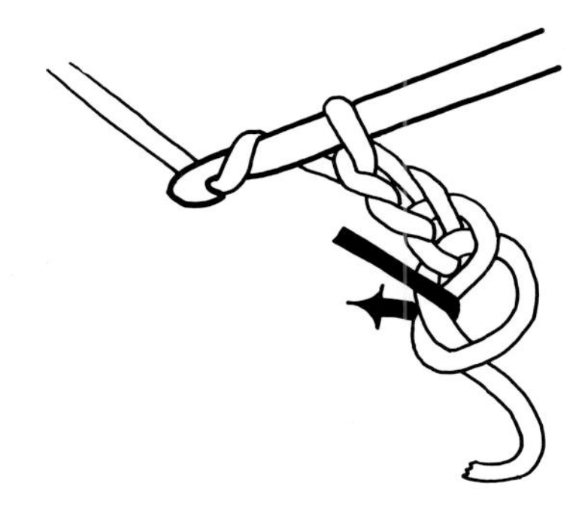

22a *Starting – slip loop method.*
Make a slip knot, but do not tighten it. Make the normal starting chain and work the stitches of the first round into the open knot. When you have finished, you can draw up the tail tightly and darn it in firmly to make a solid centre to your fabric

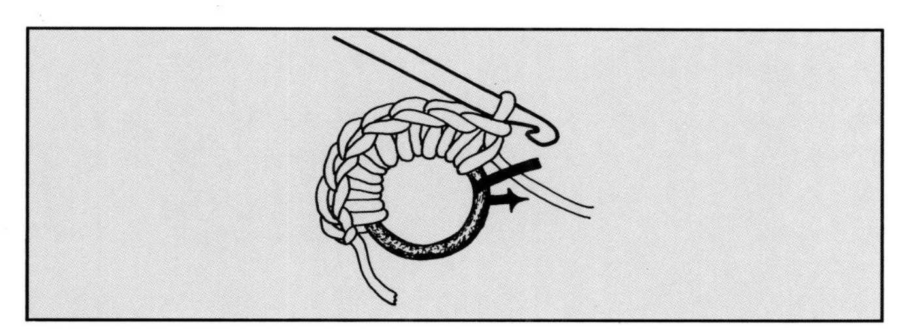

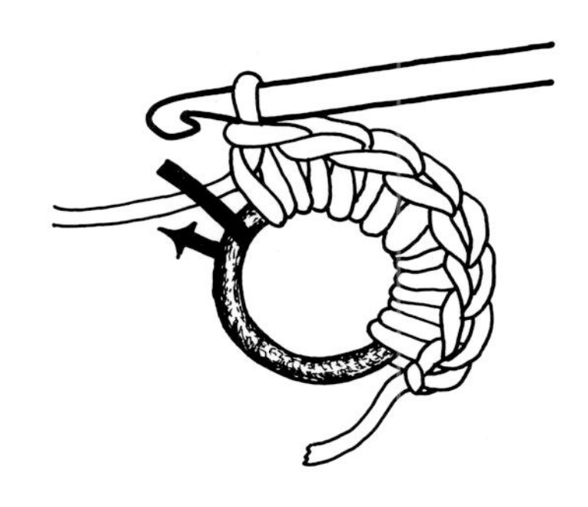

22b *Working around a ring*

it by accident often enough – but it has disadvantages: even if you mark each round it is easy to get lost and fail to increase regularly. You cannot create bands of separate colour (although multiple spirals create this illusion), or turn the fabric (which is desirable for some textured effects).

Closed rounds

This means that the end of each individual round is joined up to its own beginning and, just as in working 'to and fro', a turning or starting chain has to be worked in order to start the next round. You have the option of working each round with the same side of the fabric facing, or of turning the work between rounds.

Starting in-the-round

The standard chain ring method is most useful for tubes and flat rounds which have an open centre. The slip loop method (22a), however, allows you to draw the centre together afterwards and close up the central hole.

Whether for tubes or flat rounds, remember you can also start by working directly around a bangle, curtain or lampshade ring, etc. (22b).

Joining rounds

Joining base chain rings and rounds is easily done with a slip stitch. It may be wise, however, not to join the base chain ring of a tubular made garment into a ring until after the first round has been completed and any hidden problems have been discovered.

The orthodox way of working – joining each round with a slip stitch and then immediately working the starting chain for the next round above it – creates a clear join line in a seamless garment. You may find it worth while to disguise this by fastening off and rejoining the yarn at a different point on the round each time.

Increasing to keep spirals and closed rounds flat

If you start with too few stitches and/or increase too little as you work, your fabric will become cone or cup shaped. If you start with too many stitches and/or increase too much, it will become fluted or 'gathered' like a marine flatworm. So how do you judge the increasing in order to keep the work flat? There are two approaches and you will need both at different times.

Method 1 – mathematical

This method is best for regular, geometric shapes. Once you are familiar with it, your guesswork, even in free crochet, will be more effective.

Guidelines (23) for making solid circle, hexagons and squares with different stitches are:

1 The number of stitches needed depends upon the height of the stitch involved – the taller it is, the more stitches are required.
2 When the same stitch is used throughout, the number of stitches which has to be added is the *same* for every round and this number is the same as the number of stitches in round 1.
3 To make as perfect a circle as possible, increases should be made one by one and spaced as evenly as possible around the ring. To make other regular shapes, e.g. triangles, squares, pentagons, hexagons, etc., the increasing needs to be divided into 3, 4, 5, 6, etc., respectively, and placed at the same points on every round.

Method 2 – practical

This method is best for making organic or intuitive shapes. There are only two guidelines:

1 Test your work regularly and often by placing the fabric on a firm, flat surface, and checking it honestly.
2 Work only one stitch into each stitch until your check shows that the last stitch worked leans back far enough to enable you to put another into the same place without this one leaning forward excessively. (You will find that on round 2 this will happen on *every* stitch, but gradually becomes less often, the more rounds you work.)

Openwork

The simplest form of openwork, called filet, is a regular grid, made by substituting chains for trebles on an alternate basis. Filet patterns, which are generally presented on graph paper like cross-stitch or picture knitting charts, are created by 'filling in' some of the chain spaces with trebles.

More elaborate patterns are produced by making chain loop arches, groups (several stitches worked into the same place), clusters and using varying stitch lengths to introduce curves into the row structure. Designs resembling shells, fruit and flowers, as well as abstract and geometric traceries, are created in these ways.

Openwork in-the-round

The simplest form of openwork flat round is made of spiralling chain loops. Depending upon the number of chains in each loop and the number of loops in the first round, it lies flat *without increasing* for several rounds. (This is because the rounds become shallower.)

Generally, however, the number of stitches or pattern repeats must be increased at the same rate as for solid structures, or the size of each repeat must be enlarged in proportion. Note that the number of stitches in a round of openwork is likely to be greater as chains are used instead of other stitches.

Joining in new yarn and working with colour

To bring in a new ball of yarn when the old one is running out, make the change when there is still some of the old yarn left and you are in the middle of a stitch. Clasp the ends of both yarns under the fingers which hold the work,

23 *Flat rounds*

Stitch	*Round 1*	*Round 2 Inc every st*	*Round 3 Inc every 2nd st*	*Round 4 Inc every 3rd st*	*Round 5 Inc every 4th st*	*Round 6 Inc every 5th st*	*Every round*
Dc [US: *sc*]	6	=12	=18	=24	= 30	= 36	+ 6
Htr [US: *hdc*]	8	=16	=24	=32	= 40	= 48	+ 8
Tr [US: *dc*]	12	=24	=36	=48	= 60	= 72	+12
Dtr [US: *tr*]	18	=36	=54	=72	= 90	=108	+18
Ttr [US: *dtr*]	24	=48	=72	=96	=120	=144	+24

pick up the new one and carry on working with this. If you like, you can tie the tails of the yarns together with a neat reef knot (24a).

When joining into a new place in the fabric after fastening off elsewhere, or when the old yarn is to be carried along as a 'float' thread and brought in again later, make a slip knot in the new yarn for security (24b).

If you cannot find a way of dealing with the yarn tails while you are working, it will usually be necessary to darn them neatly into the wrong side of the fabric with a wool needle later. You may, however, be able to lay them across the tops of the stitches you are about to work over and so encase them (24c), unless your fabric is openwork and there are gaps in the 'casing'. Alternatively, if your fabric is multicoloured and textured, you can incorporate them into the body of the next stitches you make (24d).

To join in yarn of a different colour, proceed in the same way, but bear in mind one important extra thing: the working loop in crochet always becomes part of the *next* stitch you work (not of the one you have just completed). This means that to work a whole stitch in a new colour, you must always join in the new colour just *before* you work the last step of the last stitch in the old colour. When every stitch is to be a different colour (as, for instance, in a complicated graphed design), you never finish a stitch with the same yarn you started it with!

If you are going to need a yarn again, do not cut it off, but instead lead it through to the wrong side of the fabric. If it is next going to be needed further along the same row or round, either work over and encase it, or allow it to trail on the wrong side of the fabric, whilst it is temporarily not in use, and form a 'float' when you join it in later. Carrying a large number of threads – worked over or floating – can become inconvenient and spoil the feel of the fabric; in that case it may be better to join in extra yarns in different places and, as in knitted intarsia, leave them in their own areas.

All these techniques must be experimented with and judged afresh in each context. Use the ones with which you are most comfortable and which appear to do the job best.

24 *Joining in and working with colour*

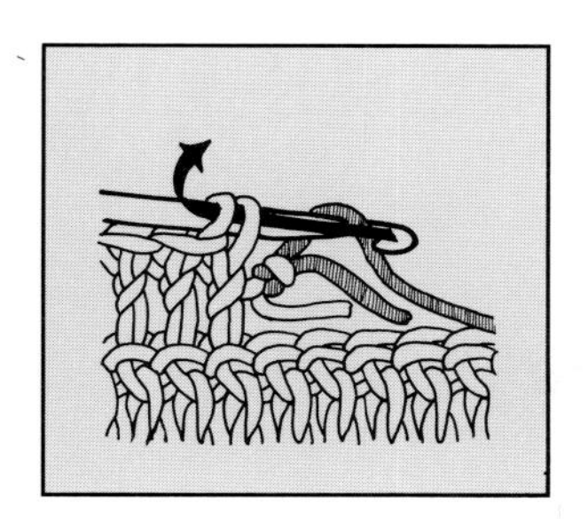

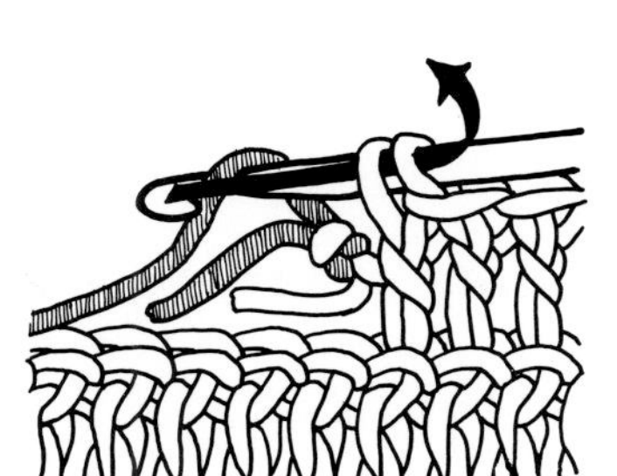

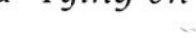

a *Tying on*

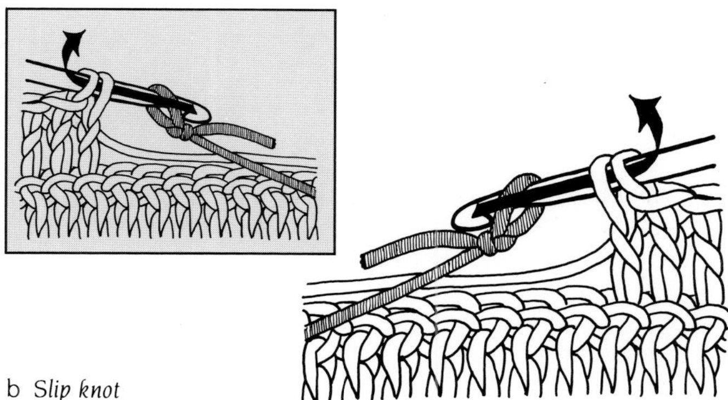

b *Slip knot*

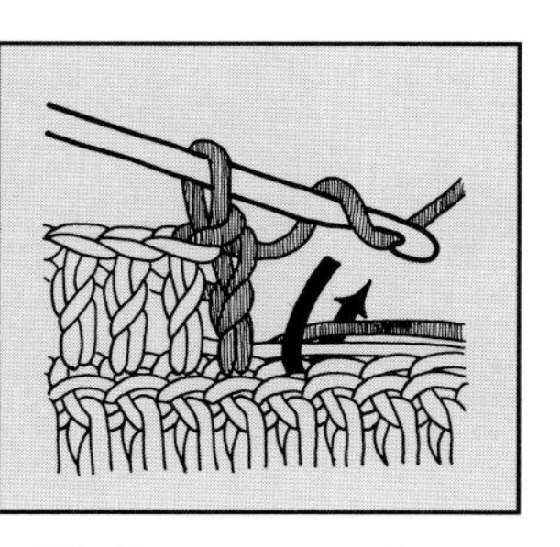

c *Working over yarn tails*

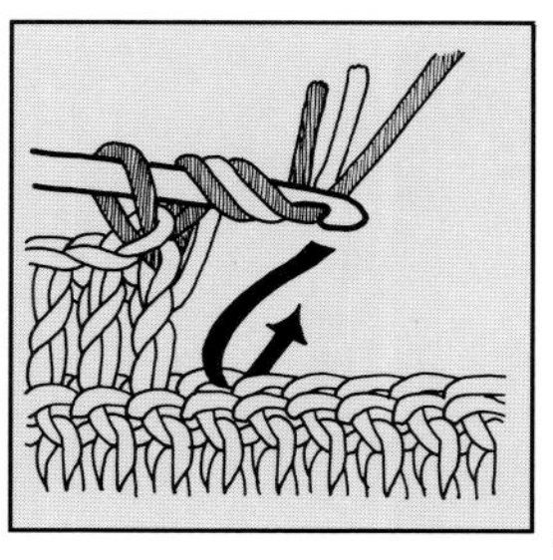

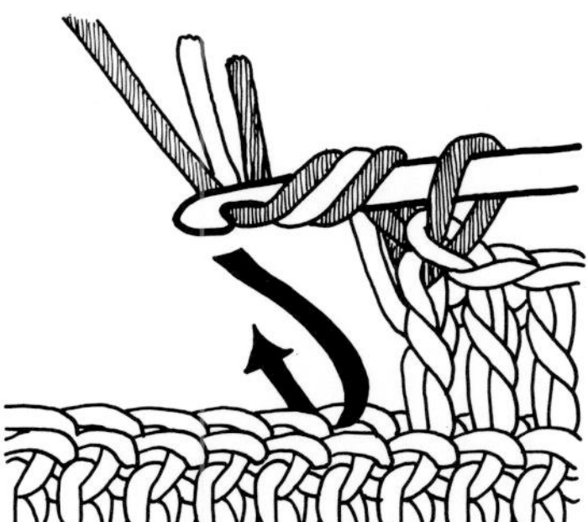

d *Incorporating yarn tails into next stitch*

Stitch developments

Once you are familiar with basic stitchmaking you may be delighted to discover that most different and exciting textured and patterned effects are produced just by varying how you insert the hook or by repeating various parts of standard procedures. By no means are all of the well-known variations described here – just some of our favourites. We strongly advise you to hunt out more and experiment for yourself to find your own new favourites, so as to make your work unique and satisfying to you.

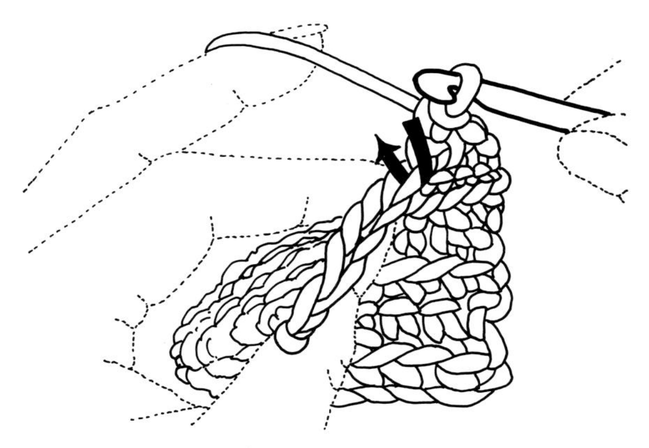

25a *Inserting the hook under the back loop only*

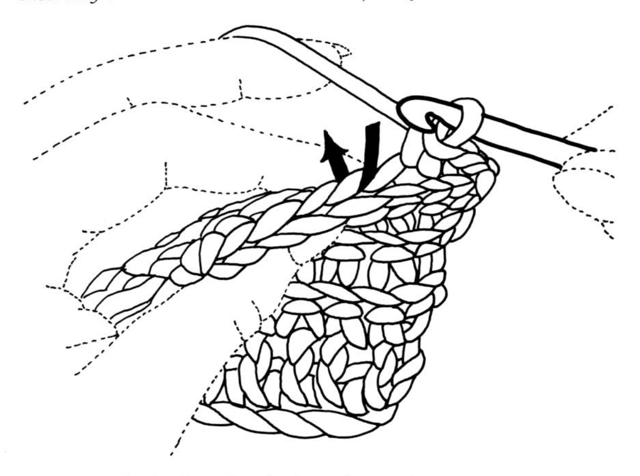

25b *Inserting the hook under the front loop only*

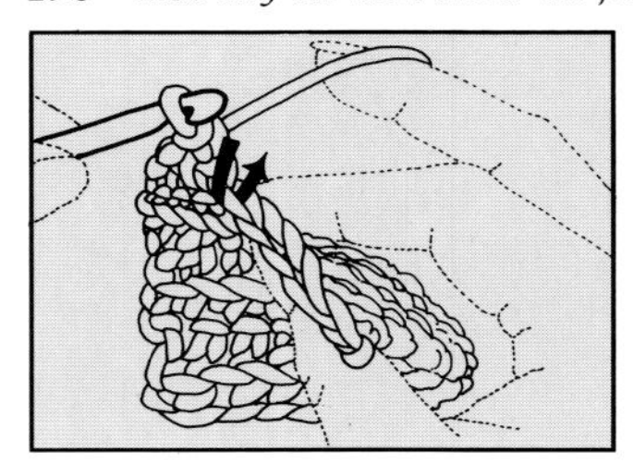

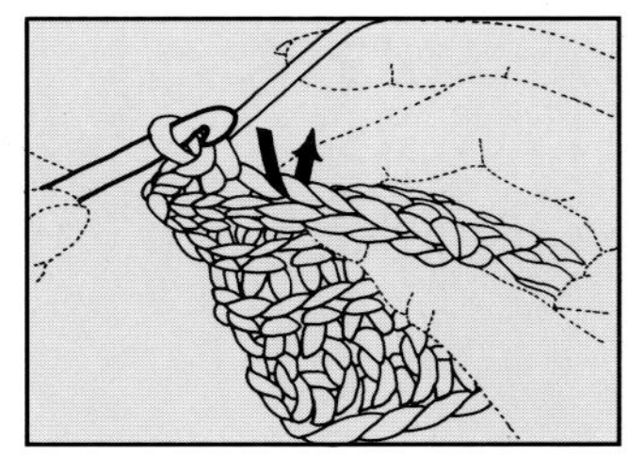

Back/front loop (25)

By inserting the hook under just one of the two loops on top of each stitch you create ridges and a more elastic fabric.

Spike (26)

A spike involves inserting the hook almost anywhere through the fabric – to a pattern or at random. It looks like blanket stitch and works best in a contrasting colour.

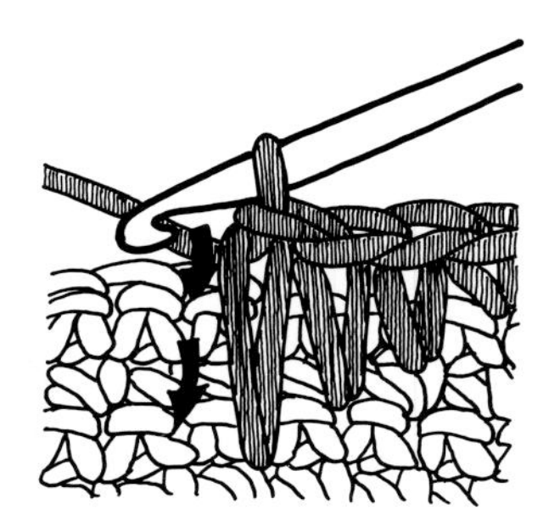

26 *Spike: Insert the hook from the front through the fabric (position varies to create different effects), yrh, draw through to the front and up loosely to the normal hook position; insert the hook as normal into the top of the next stitch in the previous row, yrh, draw another loop through the stitch only; yrh again and draw through both loops to complete*

Raised or 'round-the-stem' (27)

Stitches worked round the stem (but otherwise perfectly normally) at front or back create vertical or horizontal ridges at the front respectively – and the opposite on the other side of the fabric.

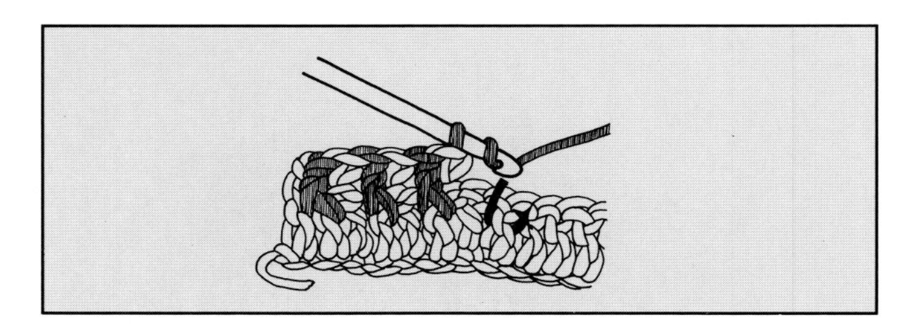

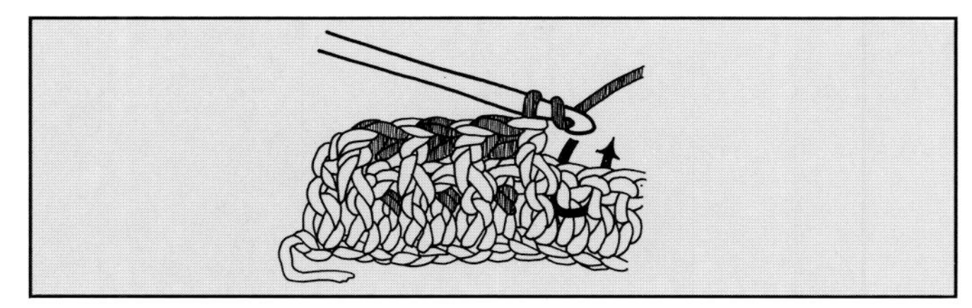

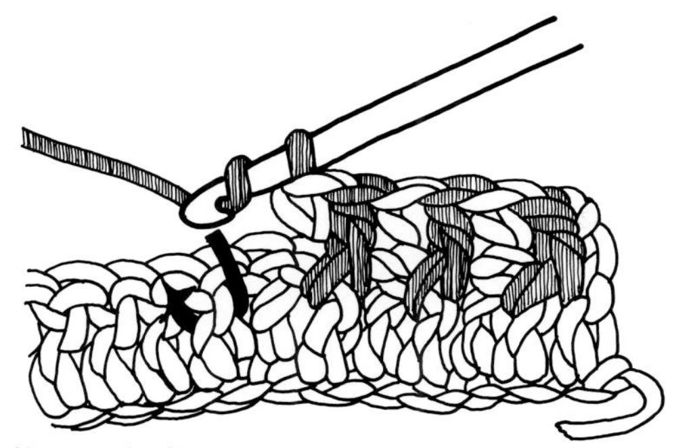

27a *Treble* |US: *double crochet*| *raised at the front* (RtrF) |US: RdcF|

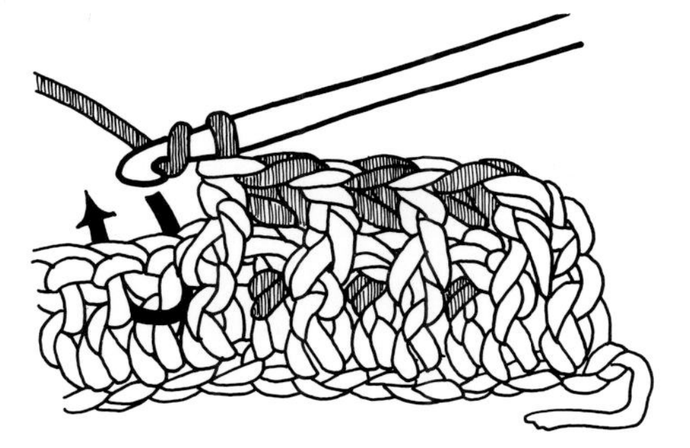

27b *Treble* |US: *double crochet*| *raised at the back* (RtrB) |US: RdcB|

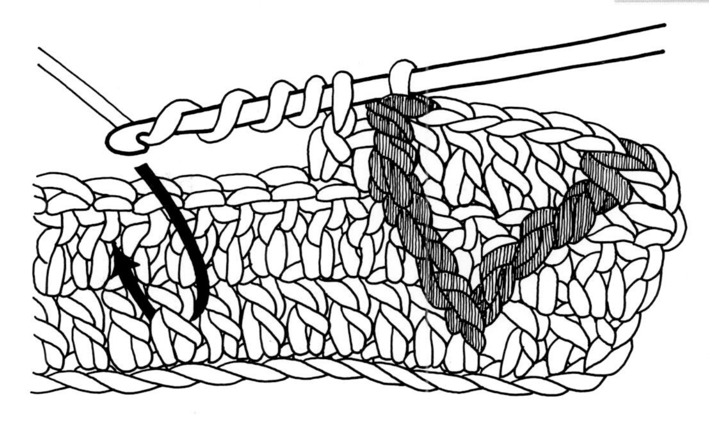

28 *Surface raised cluster*

Corded or crab stitch (29)

This is most often used as an edging, but can be used as a surface feature anywhere. It is simply the most familiar basic stitch worked in the 'wrong' direction (hence the attractive twist!).

29 *Corded or crab stitch*

1 *Insert the hook into the next stitch to the right; drop the hook on to the supply thread and draw it through the fabric (but not the loop on the hook) and up as though you were going to the left again*

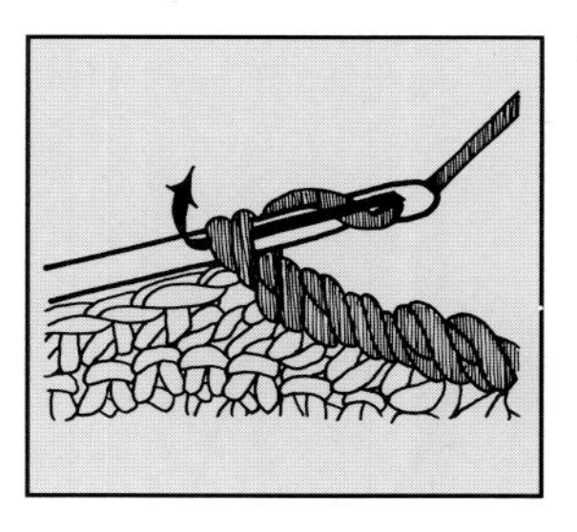

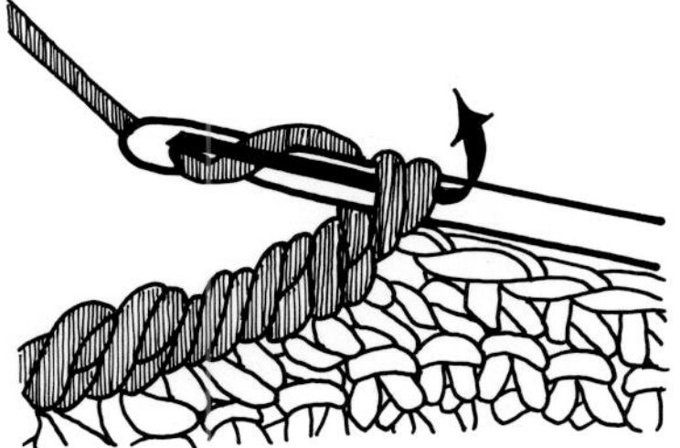

2 *Yrh, draw through both loops on the hook.* To continue: *repeat from* 1

Surface raised (28)

Raised stitches may also be worked in clusters with ordinary stitches to provide a textured relief feature. They could equally be neat and straight and part of a formal, geometric pattern, or loose and wriggly, to simulate organic root growths.

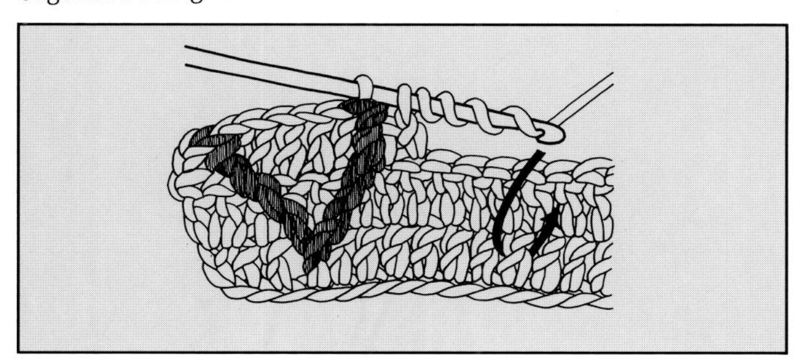

Surface crochet (30)

A technique for decorating or developing a fabric (not necessarily crochet) – maybe an afterthought or carefully considered part of the whole design. Both the methods shown are needed, sometimes in combination, for different results.

Surface slip stitch (30*a*) allows great precision and control of direction.

Full surface crochet (30*b*) enables you to build up deep texture and three-dimensional effects.

Lumps, bumps, bobbles and loops

All these stitches can be made to stand out either towards you (on right side rows) or away from you (on wrong side rows) as you complete them. They are usually most prominent when pushed out to the back.

There are plenty of variations to be tried: use more stitches and taller or shorter ones than those shown; or use stitches of different heights in the same bobble. To achieve really expressive control of texture you need to be able to vary the nature and size of bumps and bobbles.

30 *Surface crochet*

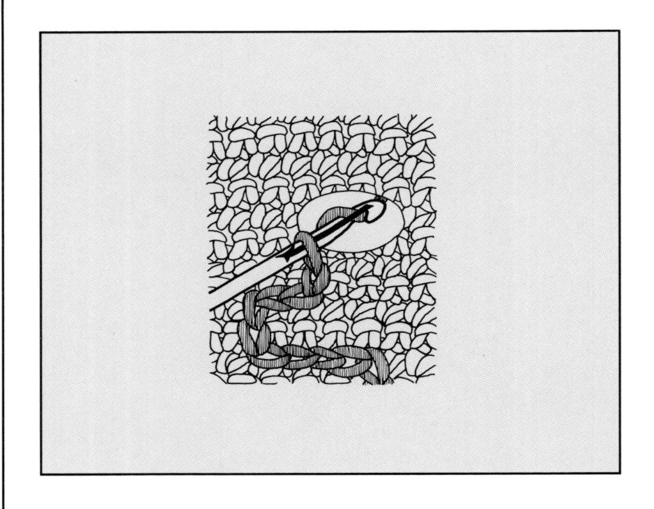

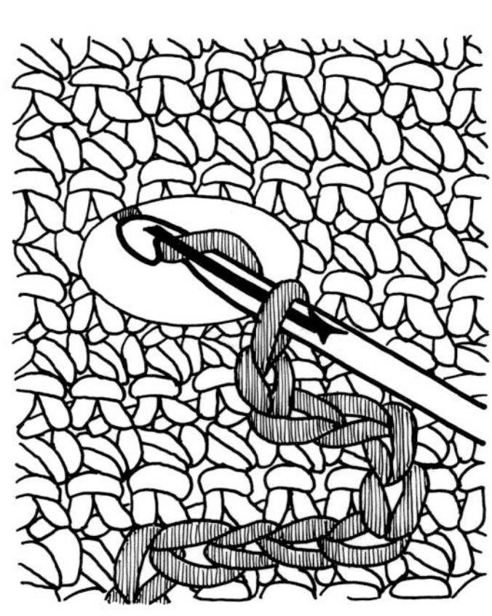

a *Surface slip stitch – with yarn at the back and hook at the front*

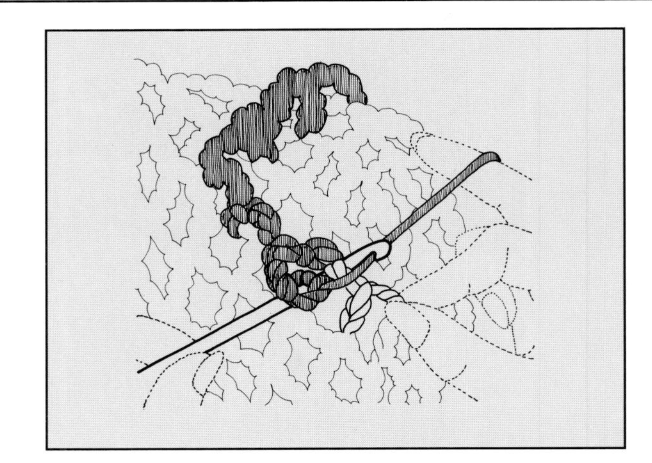

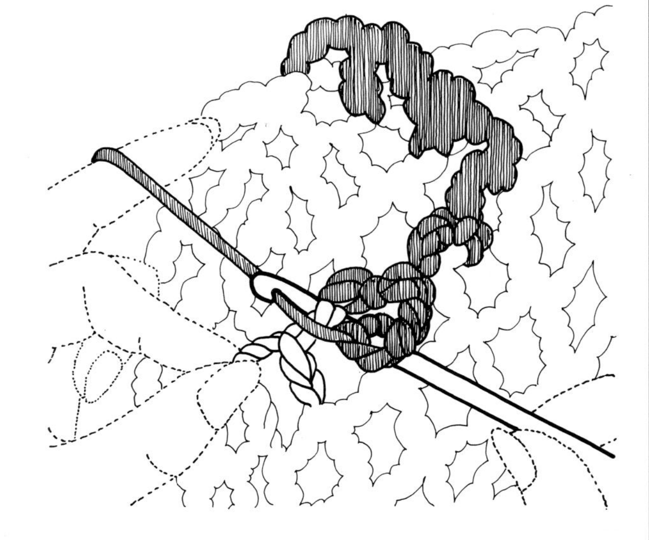

b *Full surface crochet – with hook and yarn at the front*

Bump (31)

Work any long stitch between shorter ones – the long one cannot stand up and so it bends over and sticks out. A more substantial bump is made by making a long stitch (say, dtr or ttr |US: tr or dtr|) as a cluster with, say, a dc or tr |US: sc or dc|.

Popcorn (32)

Work a complete group of long stitches into the same place, take the hook out of the working loop, insert it through the top of the first stitch of the group (from front or back, depending upon which way the popcorn is required to stick out), pick up the old working loop again and draw through.

31 *Bump*

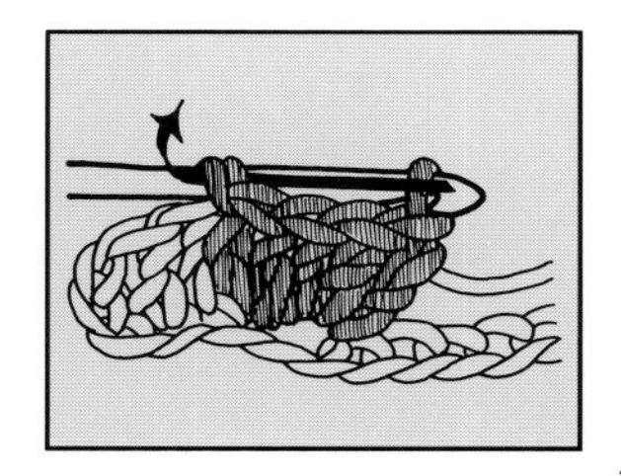

32 *Popcorn*

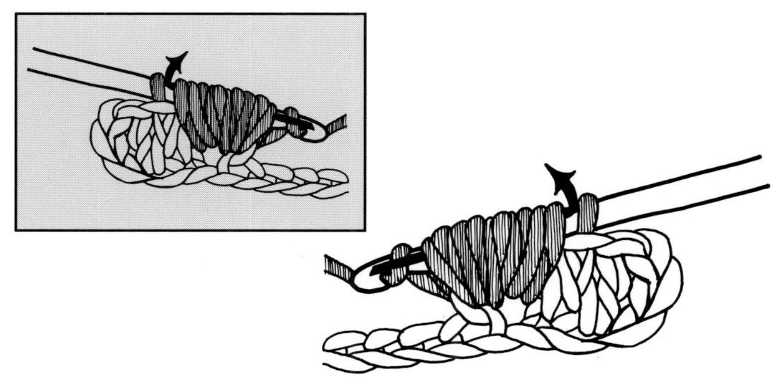

33 *Puff stich. To finish: yrh, draw through last 2 loops*

Puff stitch (33)

A puff stitch is a treble |US: dc| in which the first three stages (yrh, insert hook, yrh and draw through fabric) are repeated up to five times (perhaps even more).

Bobble (34)

The classic bobble is a cluster of 5 trebles |US: double crochet| worked into the same place. Usually double |US: single| crochets are worked on either side to make the cluster more prominent.

Bullion stitch (35)

This starts as an ordinary long stitch (yrh 8, 10 or more times) for stages 1 to 3, then becomes a coiled tube when stage 4 is drastically contracted.

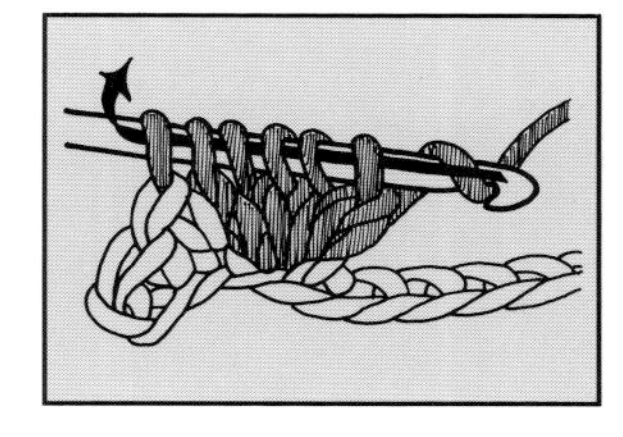

34 *Bobble (a cluster with all stitches worked into the same place)*

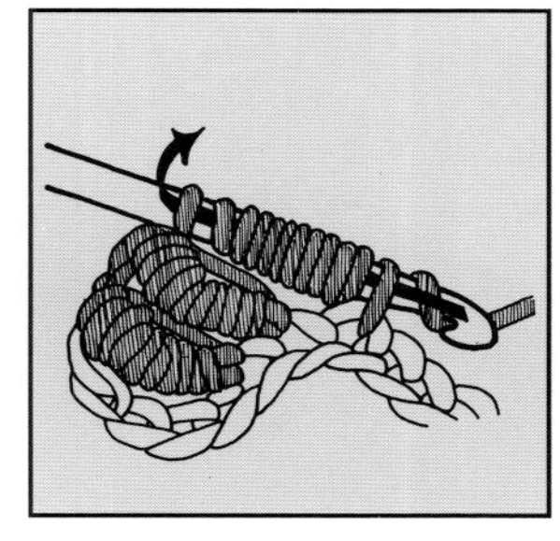

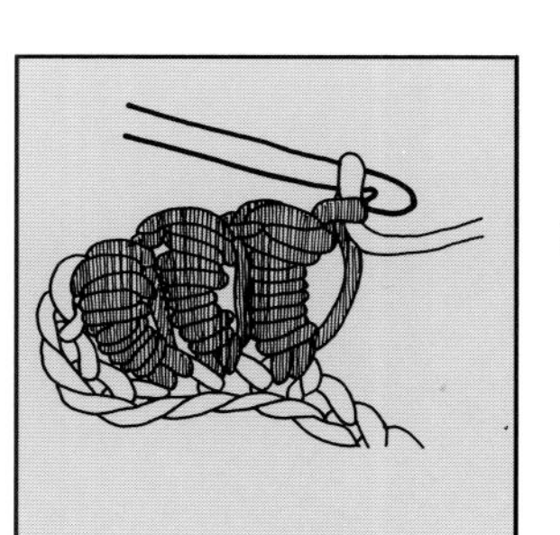

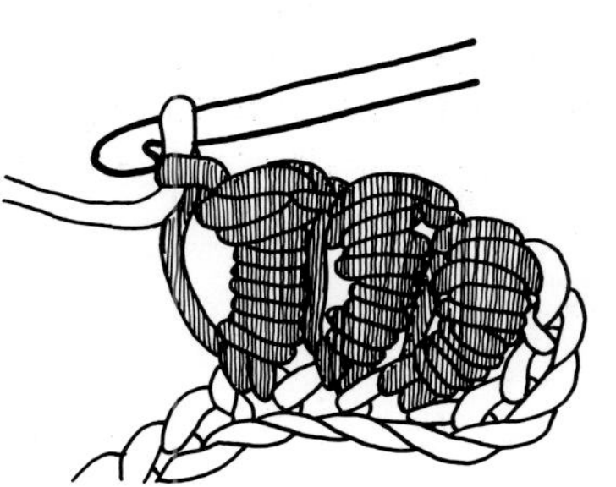

35 *Bullion stitch. You need to pick off the loops one by one. To finish: make 1ch to bring the supply thread up to the top of the stitch*

Loop (fur) stitch (36)

Be careful to make the loops as shown, or they may pull out very easily – which will be especially bad news if you have already cut them!

36 *Loop/fur stitch – based on double [US: single] crochet*

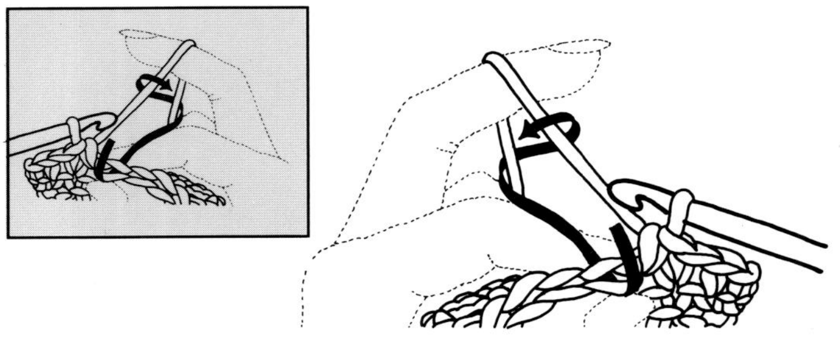

1 *Insert the loop, reach through and pick up the supply thread on the far side of your tension finger*

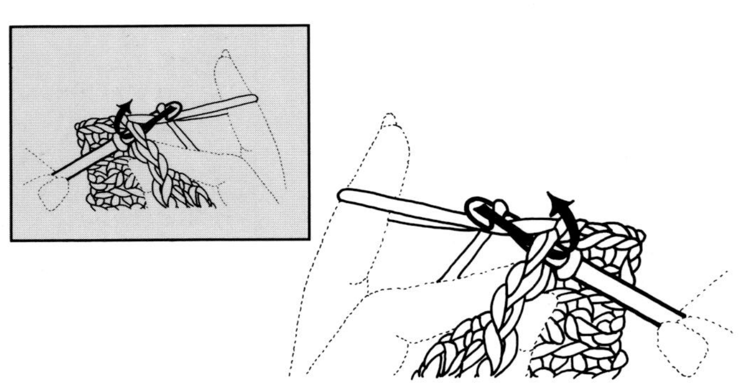

2 *Draw this back and at the same time pick up the first part of the supply thread; pull both threads through the fabric*

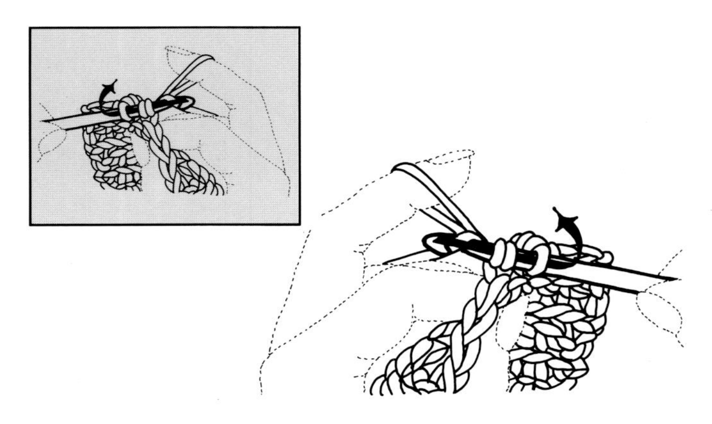

3 *Yrh, draw through all three loops on the hook; take your finger out of the finished loop*

Solomon's knot (37)

Solomon's knots provide a wonderful way of showing off yarns. You can use different yarns together.

37 *Solomon's knot*

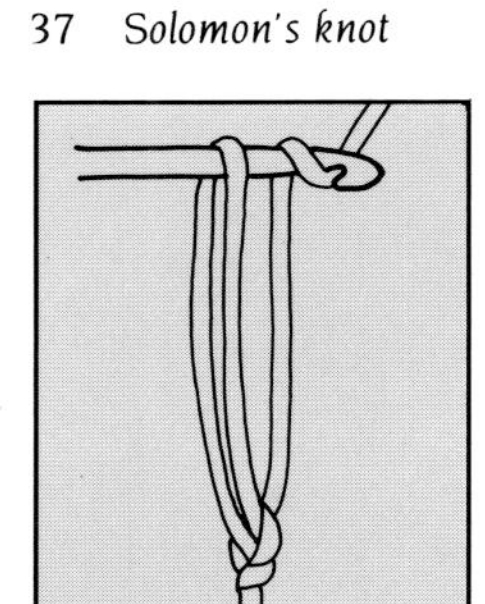

1 *Make 1ch and draw out the loop to length required; yrh and prepare to pull the new loop through . . .*

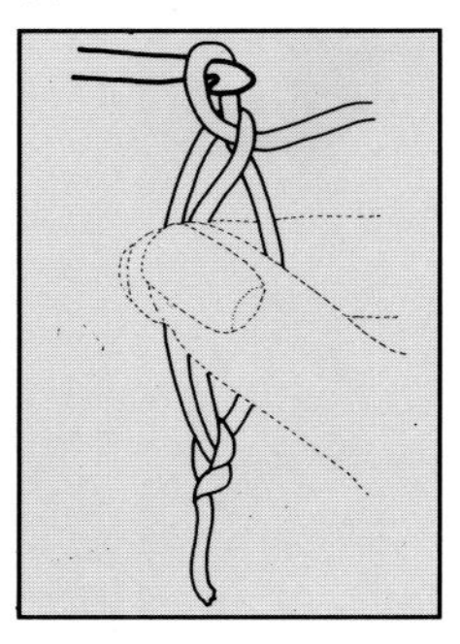

2 *. . . but, before you do, change your left hand grip and hold the single rear thread apart from the two front ones, so that you can insert the hook under the back thread . . .*

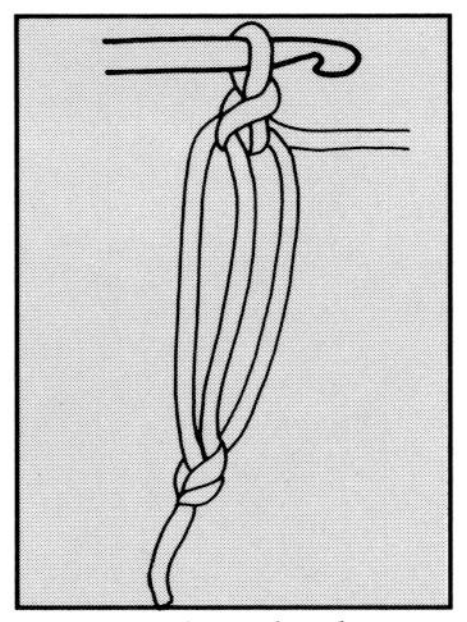

3 *. . . and work 1dc [US: 1sc] to 'lock' the Solomon's knot*

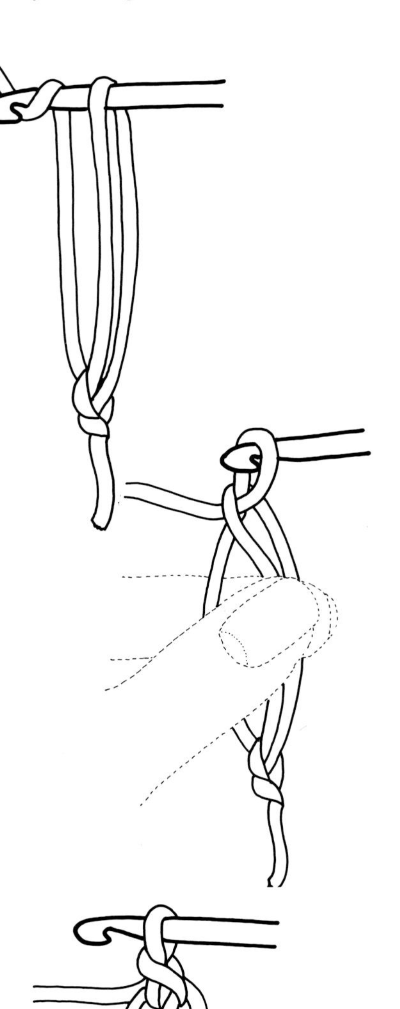

3
Free-form crochet

Crochet is more like needlepoint and painting than knitting or weaving in that it lends itself to 'doodling' – filling a space by adding a little at a time here and there – rather than scanning to and fro in straight lines across a rectangle like a computer or television screen. It is amazing that this wonderful potential has hardly been exploited since the Irish crochet lacemakers built up their astonishing compositions in the last century.

Once you are happy about making a base chain and working back and forth or round and round, using the basic stitches, you are ready to start making some exciting crochet fabrics. We dare you to come with us, to tiptoe gently from the straight and narrow (and those ever-increasing circles) into fields where the grass is greener . . . and redder, and bluer and so lush as to give the word texture a whole new meaning!

Before we abandon the conventional row or round structure completely, however, let us look at some ways to use it to make interesting and irregular effects.

Irregular curves and zigzags

Increasing and decreasing during rows can produce chevrons and curves. Conventionally this is done regularly and evenly, but it need not always be (38).

Varying stitch height

Stitch height can be varied to create wave patterns. The fabric stays reasonably flat, if shorter stitches are always worked over longer stitches and vice versa on a compensating basis (39, 40). We can take that idea further by making randomly shaped non-repeating waves (41, 42), which are so easy to create spontaneously as you work that there is no need to plan them in advance on paper, unless you have some specific grand design in mind.

In order to sort out your 'opposites', decide on the longest and shortest stitches you are going to use and plot the stages in between.

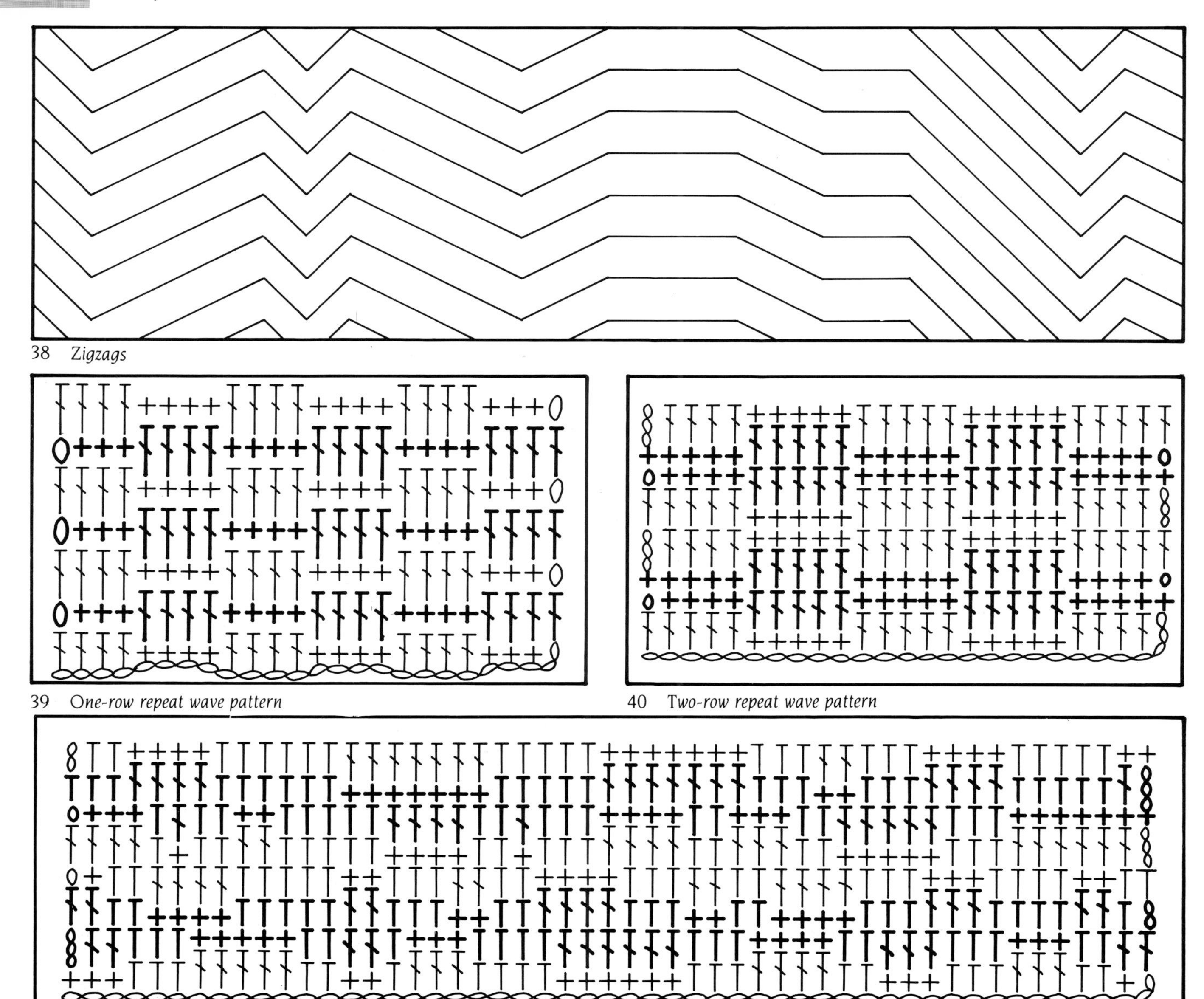

38 *Zigzags*

39 *One-row repeat wave pattern*

40 *Two-row repeat wave pattern*

41 *'Random' waves. For a very wobbly effect, which disguises the straight lines of the row structure, always work two whole rows with the same colour. On the first row with each new colour you 'straighten' the waves you have just made (if you are working spontaneously, just look at the stitch you are about to work into and do the 'opposite'). On the second row you create a new series of waves*

42 'Random' waves (vertical rows): *this fabric is made exactly as described in 41 and, for maximum effect, the yarns are all of different textures and space-dyed in many colours.*

43 *Light random texture: stitch anarchy, using only basic stitches*

Bubbles and bulges

If varying stitch height is used without sufficient compensation, the waves can become three-dimensional bubbles and bulges (44). You can make these even more pronounced with some judicious increasing and decreasing.

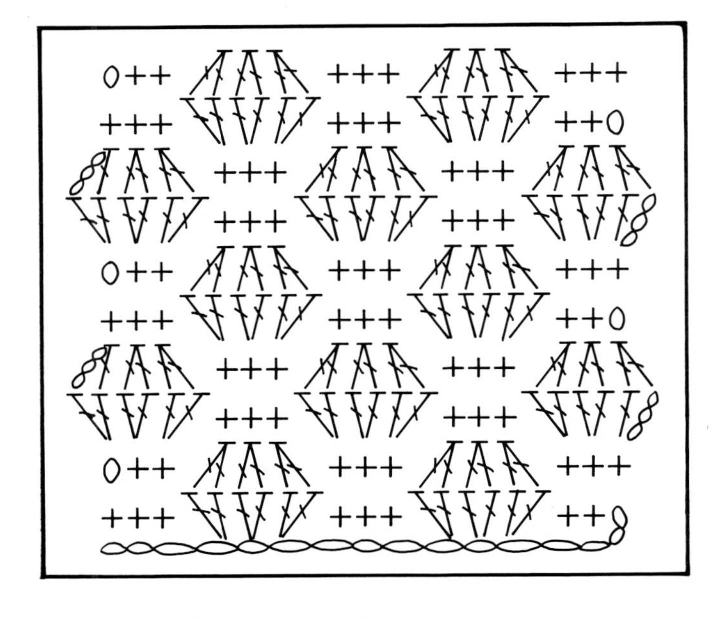

44 *Bubbles and bulges: the decreasing should compensate for the increasing (and vice versa), so long as you want no overall 'shaping' to the fabric. Notice that the diagram has to be drawn distorted in order to lie flat!*

Light texture

What happens if you work stitches of different height *totally at random*? Why not try it – it gives a more textured fabric in which the row structure is less obviously defined (43).

Only decide which stitch you are going to work as you start to make it. Hardly ever work the same type of stitch twice running. Avoid neat waves, repeat sequences and any compensating with 'opposites'.

Slivers and wedges

As soon as you begin to realise that you do not *always* have to work the whole way across every row, or complete every round, you are taking the next step towards free-form crochet! Still without abandoning the essential row (or round) structure, see how you can turn your waves into slivers (45, 46).

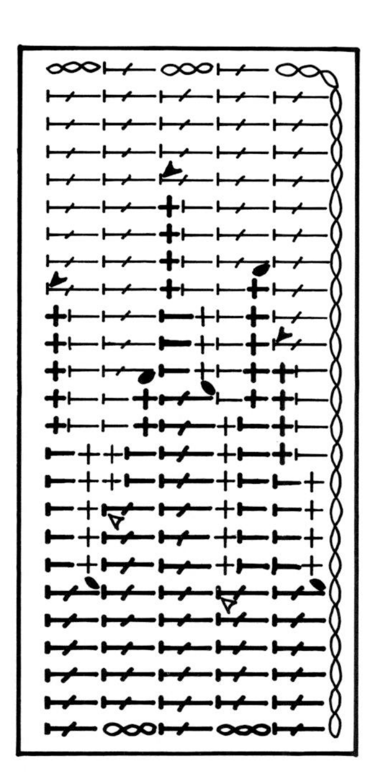

45 Slivers and wedges: using two colours per row and a regular row structure, taper off the first colour with a succession of shorter stitches, then, to maintain the required row height, work 'opposites' to begin the second colour. **NB** *Join the second colour into the top of the last full length stitch worked with the first colour, i.e. at symbol:* △ ▲

46 Only two colours are used here and there is only one transition from colour to colour in each row; you could have several transitions and never repeat a colour

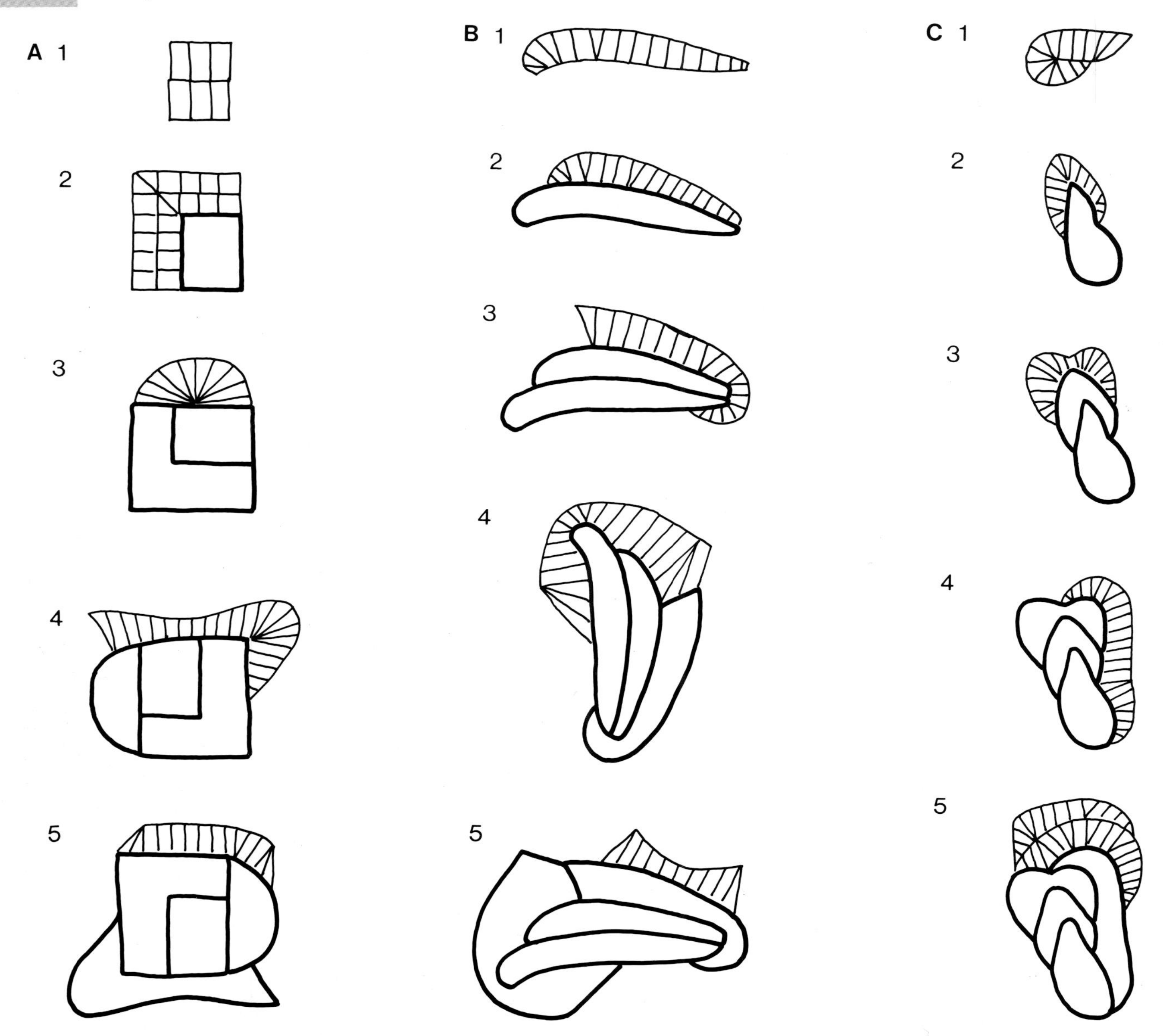

47 *Starting to 'doodle'*

Starting to 'doodle'

Quite soon it is possible to forget all idea of regular rows or rounds and add slivers, wedges and chunks, waves or bulges anywhere you fancy. By then you are beginning to 'doodle' properly – but now how do you start? Your usual ways will probably be to make just two or three chains and part of a circle or a short row. Now that you are no longer restricted to working into the tops of previous stitches, these beginnings can develop in subtly interesting or wildly surprising ways, depending upon the project and your imagination (47, 48a).

48b

48a

Lace openwork

Openwork can also be worked freely. It may be more important to keep the work flat, so more skill and care may be needed (48b).

Texture

As soon as you have become familiar with textured stitches and stitchmaking techniques (working into the back or front loop only, spikes, raised stitches, popcorns, puff stitches, bobbles, bullion stitches, loop stitch, etc.) you are free to introduce these into free-form doodles, if the project theme suggests them (49).

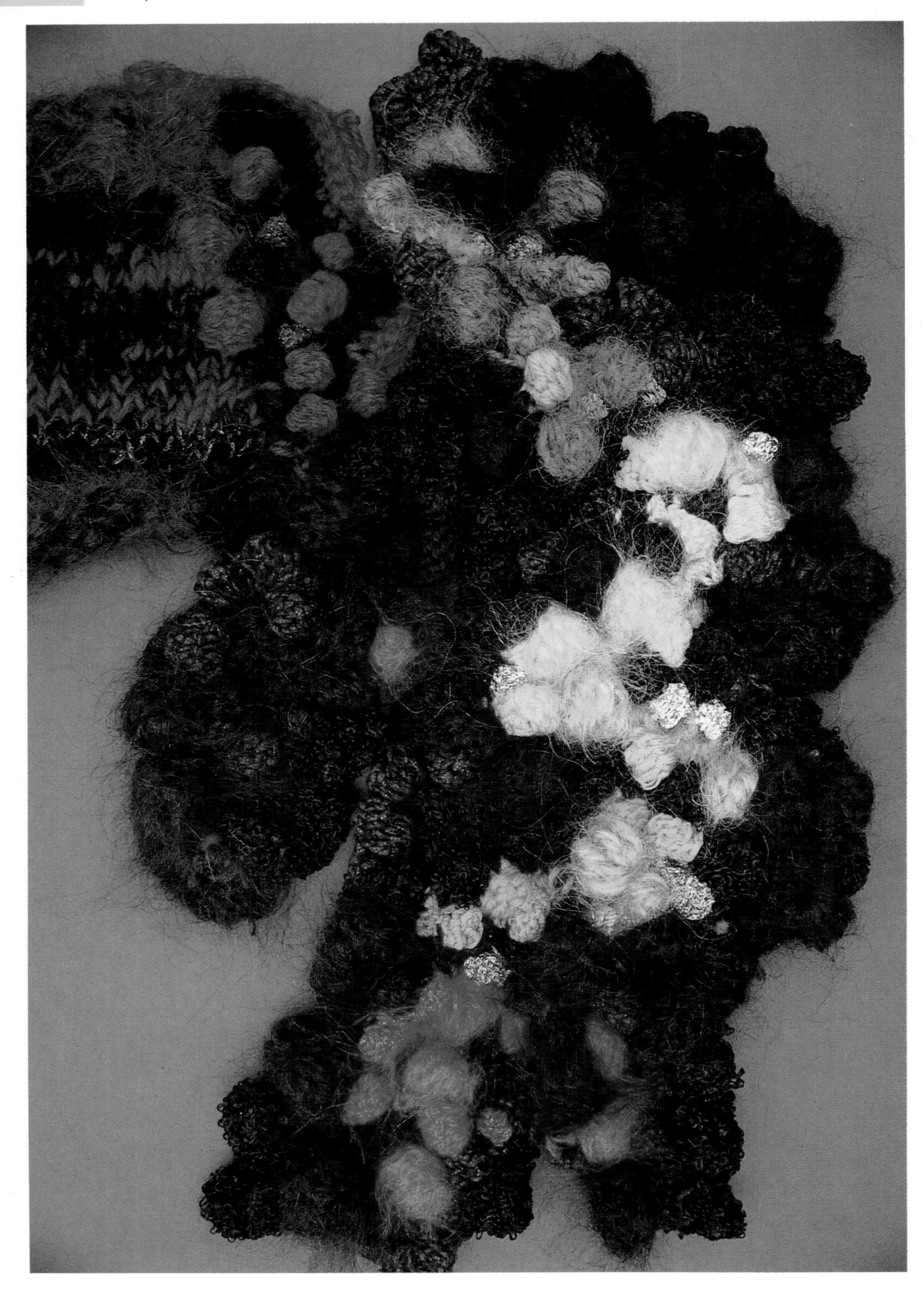

49

Free-form 'doodling'

Our general advice is:

1. Use lots of colours and texture, change yarn often and work only a few stitches with each.
2. Use treble [US: dc] as the basic stitch unit, switching to shorter or taller stitches to create slivers and wedges, to smooth out dips and to build up straight edges.
3. Be aware of which are to be the right and wrong sides of your fabric, so that your surface texture appears where you need it.
4. Incorporate all yarn tails into the stitches or work over and encase them whenever possible (otherwise they will all have to be darned in afterwards).

Technical guidelines

You can learn nothing without doing it yourself, but then there is nothing that you cannot teach yourself, if you are prepared to experiment.

1. In order to work evenly (unless you want to create a bulge, gather, curve or other change of direction), work one stitch per stitch over the tops (or bottoms) of previous stitches. Knowing how many stitches to work over the ends of rows needs judgement, which feeds on practice (50). Here is a rough guide to working over straight row ends – you will sometimes need to adjust it according to circumstances (angles, hook size, yarn quality, individual stitch gauge, etc.):

Over row end	Work
Dc [US: sc]	1 stitch
Htr [US: hdc]	1 stitch and 2 stitches alternately
Tr [US: dc]	2 stitches
Dtr [US: tr]	3 stitches

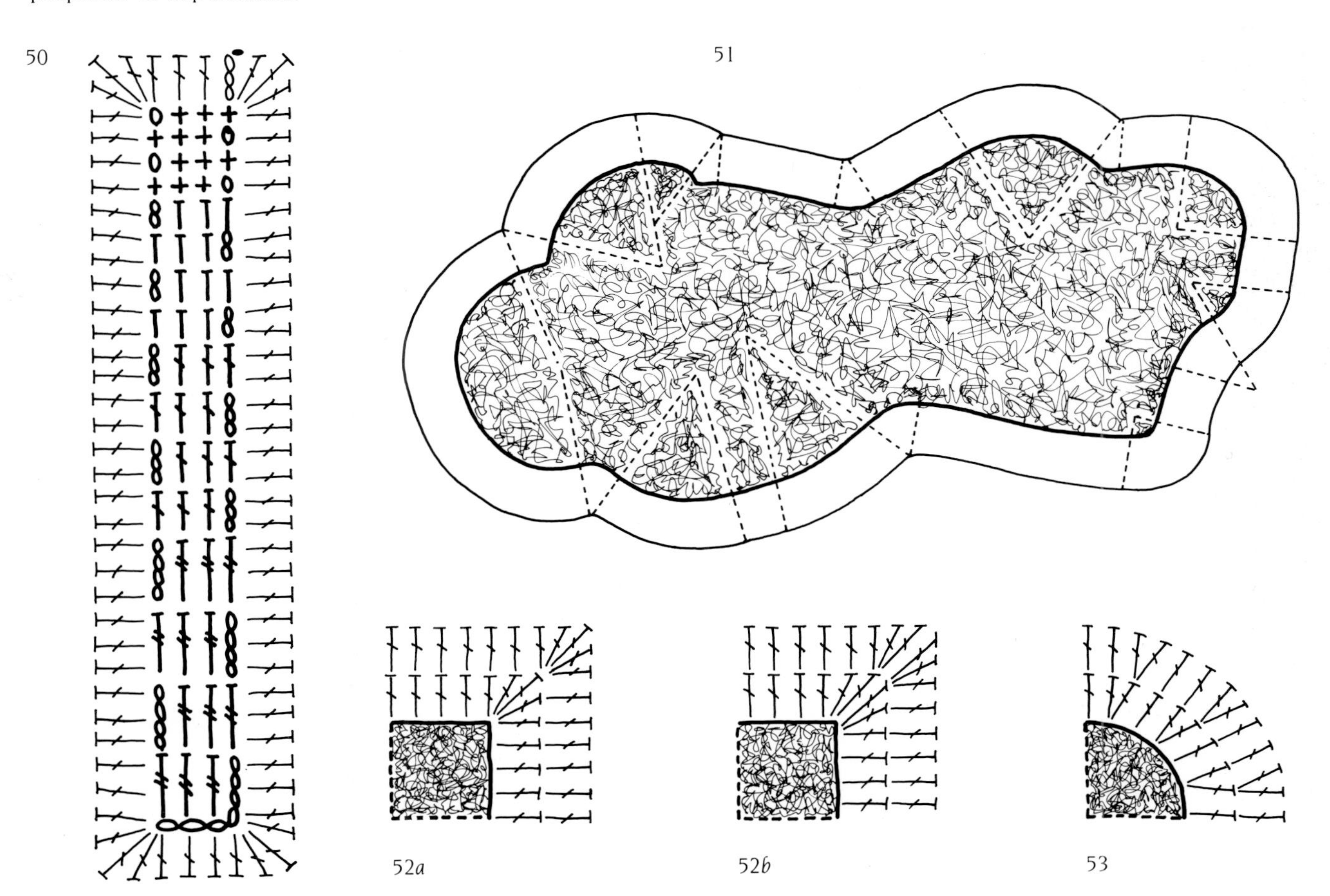

50

51

52*a*

52*b*

53

2 When working over a row end, you have to 'invent' a place to insert the hook. Pick up at least two threads of the edge stitch – going first into what was the top of it (the same place as the base of the next edge stitch) and then, in the case of the longer stitches, into the stem.

3 In order to go around corners and curves:
a Concentrate on sizing up how much of a whole circle the corner or curved section goes through (51). This is often much less than you think. Then remember that you need to increase 12 times to go the whole way around a circle using treble stitches (less often for shorter stitches and more often for longer ones – see chapter 2).
b A square corner (52) is a quarter circle and so needs 4 increases, which could be worked as 5 stitches into the corner or 3 stitches twice (either side of the corner).
c A regular curve covering the same quarter circle (53) needs the same 4 increases, but regularly and evenly spaced.
d When you are working around the inside of a corner or curve, you must expect to decrease by similar amounts (54).
e Smaller angles require fewer increases or decreases (55).

4 Varying stitch height:
a If you are building up an edge by using taller stitches (56), be prepared to increase as well – your new edge is going to be longer than the old one.
b Be prepared to decrease when you are filling in (57).
c Gradually tapered slivers and wedge shapes (58) usually require very little increasing/decreasing.

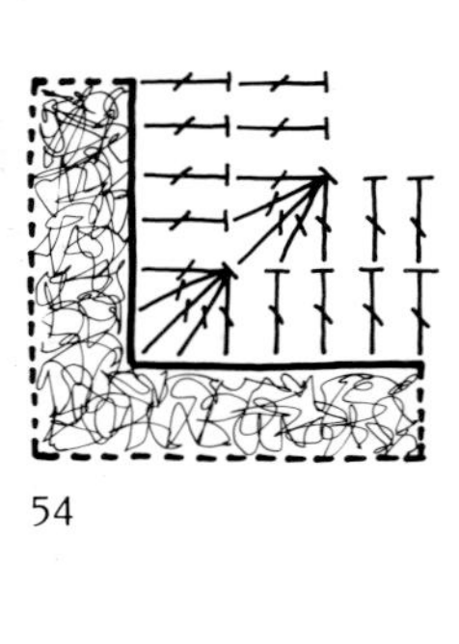

54

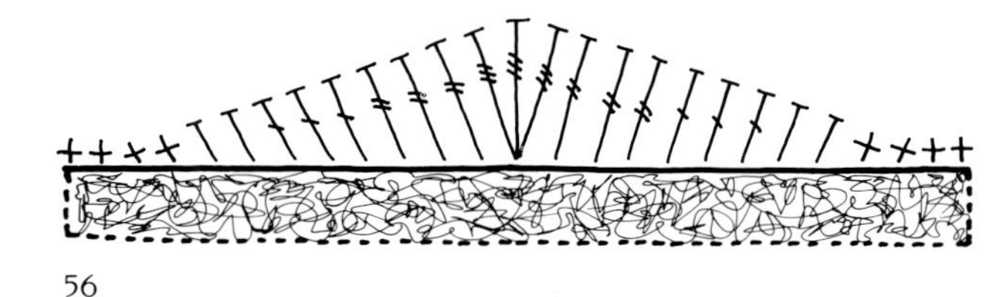

56

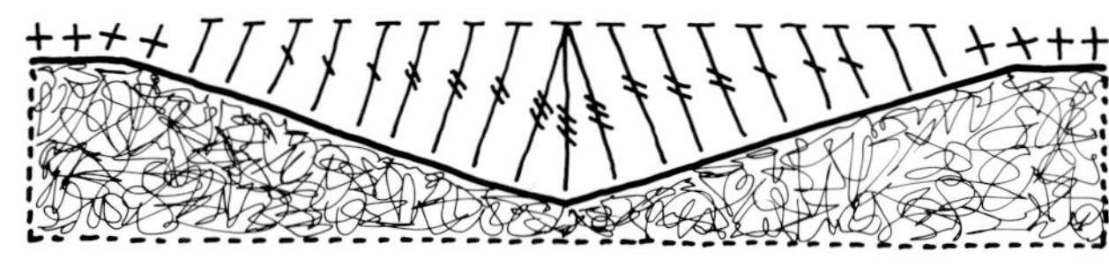

57

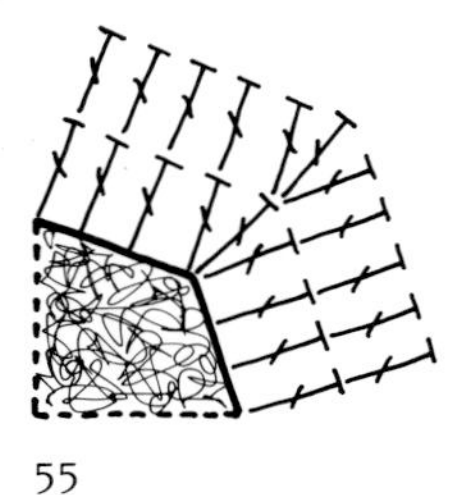

55

58

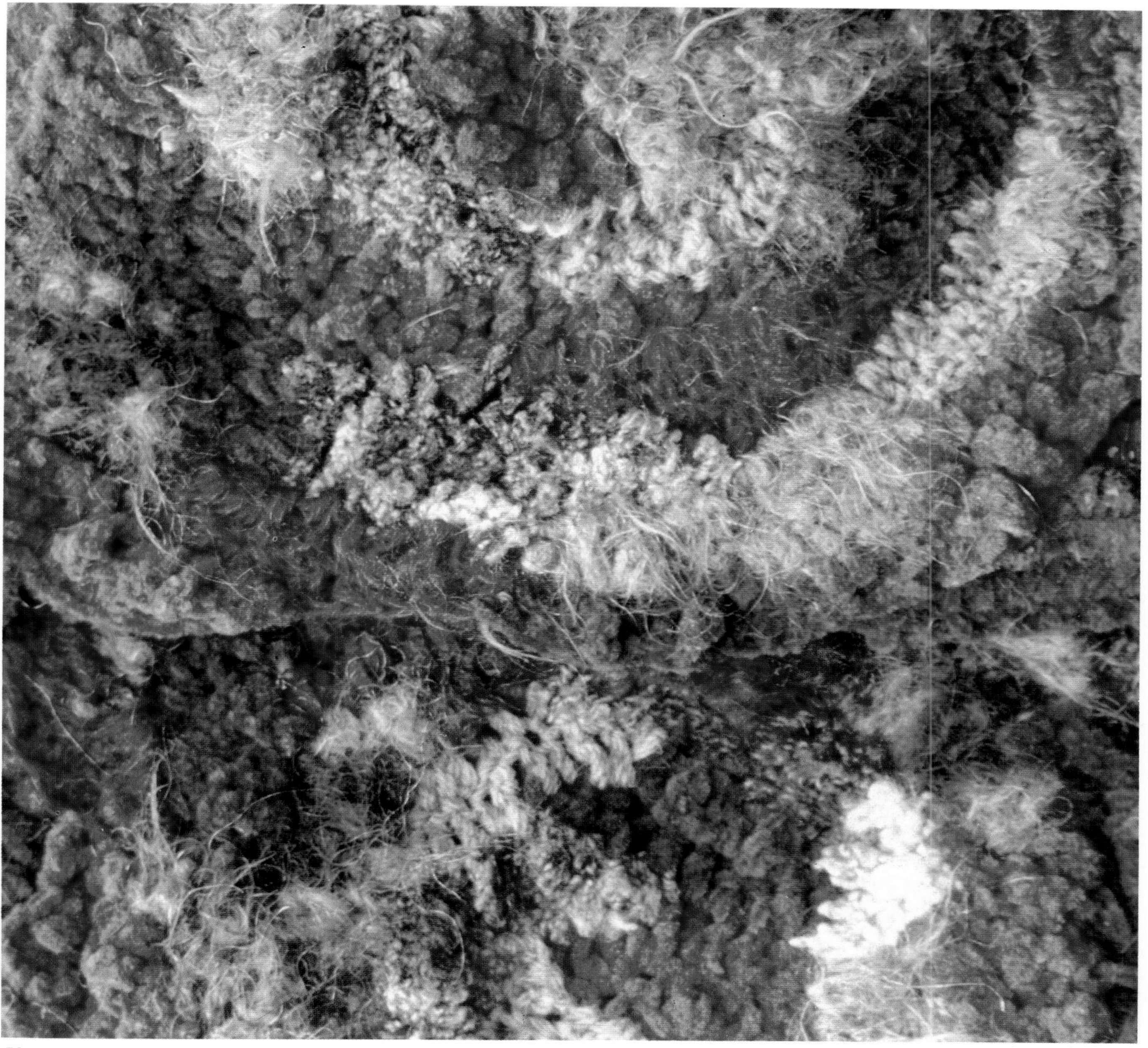

59

5 Target practice: whenever you start with a small blob and try to build it up all round, there is a strong tendency to maintain a roughly circular shape as the blob gets bigger and bigger. Even when you are certainly not working in conventional rounds, the fabric looks more and more like a melted target. If this tendency is not going to enhance your design, you should create corners and bulges, spurs, shoots and branches – remember double and treble chains [US: single crochet and double crochet chains]. Resist the constant temptation to smooth things over or round things off. Stop at frequent intervals and start new pieces – by then you are getting into free patchwork (59).

A textured 'scrumble'

To lead yourself gently into textured free-form you could start by trying our example (exactly, if necessary) several times in completely different yarns (60). Do not stop: make several additions to each one, but always in different ways, just to prove to yourself how easy it is to work in this way – and, indeed, to invent your own ways of starting in the first place.

If you have no time to make large-scale fabrics, your 'scrumbles' (61a) could turn into decorative panels and be mounted in rings or on panels and perhaps framed or sewn on to a sweater or coat. A single 'scrumble' or group of small ones could be shaped into a beret (61b).

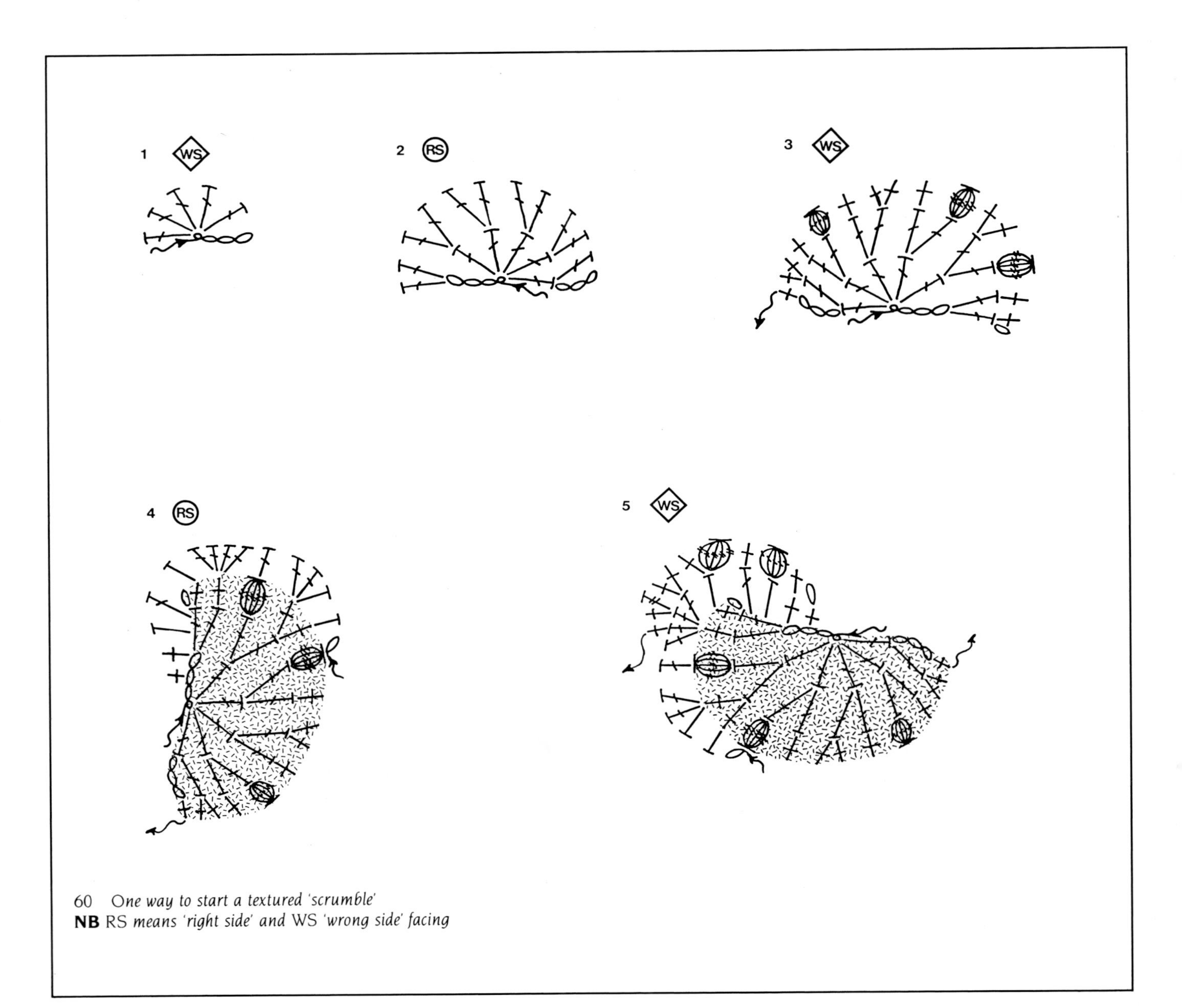

60 *One way to start a textured 'scrumble'*
NB RS *means 'right side' and* WS *'wrong side' facing*

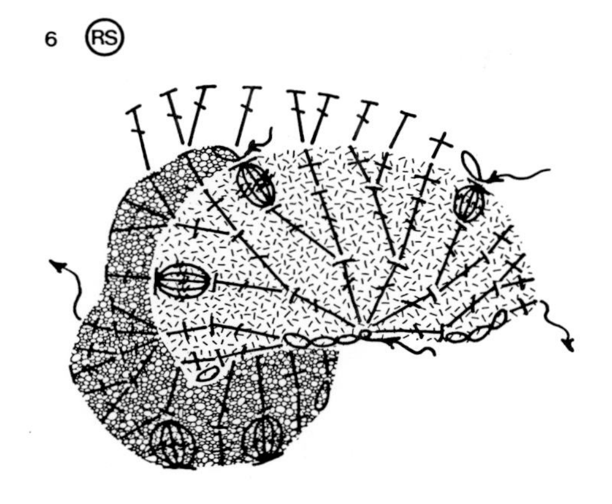
6
RS

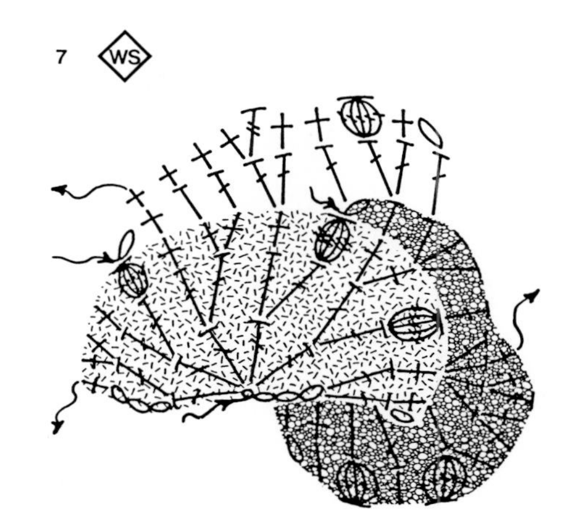
7
WS

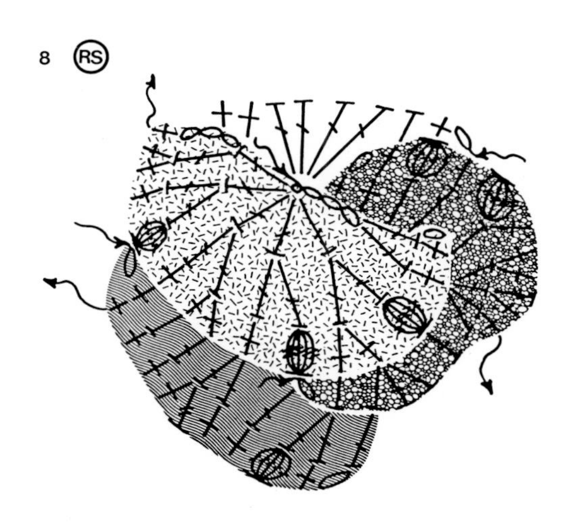
8
RS

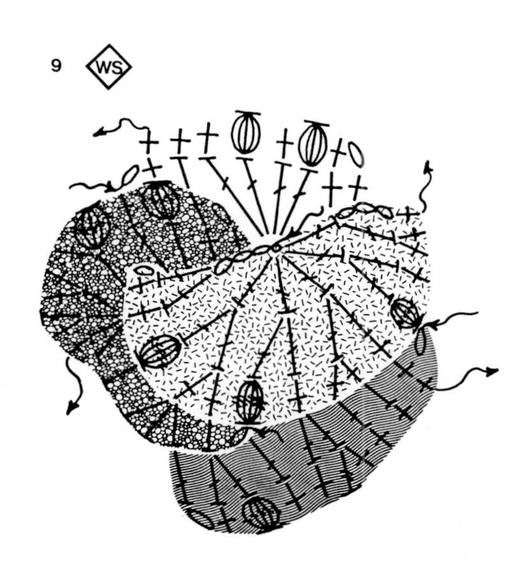
9
WS

61a *Three pieces of textured 'scrumble' . . .*

61b *. . . made up into a beret*

Representational free-form

Naturally if your fabric is to some extent representational – of a visual impression or even of a feeling – the way you work will be designed to express that. A ploughed field (62b), for instance, will involve working ridges in straight (not necessarily parallel) lines; distant hills in a landscape (62c) may require a smooth fabric in which the rows of crochet curve. Winter trees may be represented in surface crochet. To achieve the effect of a cloudy sky (62a) you might make the patches of sky plain, blue and smooth; the clouds, by contrast, would be grey and white, full of puffs and bobbles, and they would overlap both each other and the sky.

62a Cloudy sky (detail)

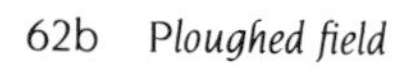

62b Ploughed field

62c Hills in a landscape

63

Crochet 'consequences'

If you are working in a group, both beginners and those experienced in crochet can have fun playing 'Crochet Consequences' (63). Everybody finds three or four balls of yarn with different textures (but related colour). They sit in a circle and each start their own tiny piece of free-form crochet. After every few minutes, they stop, fasten off and hand their piece to the next person . . . and so on. The idea is to add something small, interesting and different each time!

As people become quicker and more confident, you can reduce the time allowed. For variety (and to get your own back!), you can reverse the direction of passing the pieces around. Above all make sure everybody learns as much as possible from each other by looking carefully at all the individual pieces separately and by making their own temporary arrangement of all the finished pieces together. (If you have a camera, everyone can have a permanent record of their composition.)

64 *Controlled free-form. Textured 'scrumbling' is surprisingly easy to master and then it is not long before you can work large areas of the free-form crochet fabric with control*

Shaping up

However spontaneous your free-form doodling, it usually has to be made to fit some outline. It is indispensable to have a template made of some stable material (say, an old sheet or blanket), on which you can draw the outline and any aspects of the design you want. Then you can safety-pin the free-form pieces to the template, study the result, perhaps move the pieces into a better arrangement and finally look at how best to fill in the spaces (65).

Luckily, you will probably have already learned the necessary skills quite naturally through your doodling. You will have become familiar with roughly what to expect when you work this or that combination of stitches in a particular place, and you will now be able to guess what to try first. Working by guesswork for a few stitches at a time and being prepared to try again is much quicker than you might have thought, and very reliable when the completed pieces stay fixed in position.

One way of filling in by adding on is to use the smallest stitches all the time and work part rows (66a). We have found, however, that it is usually more convenient to use treble [US: double crochet] as the basic stitch unit and switch to stitches which are one or two stages either shorter or taller, to smooth out a dip or build up a straight edge (66b, 67, 68).

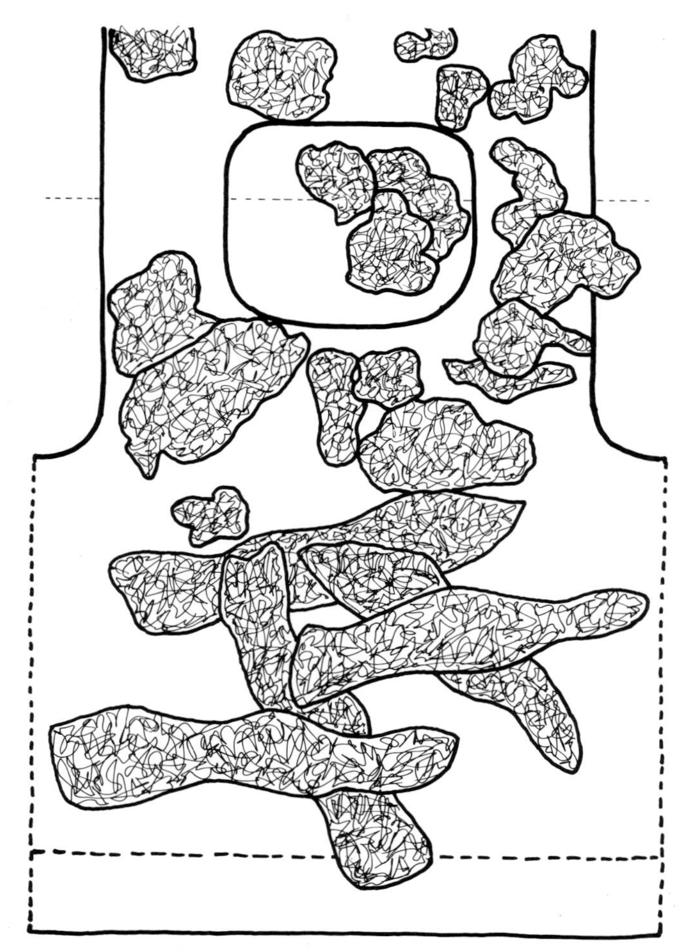

65a *Crochet the free-form pieces . . .*

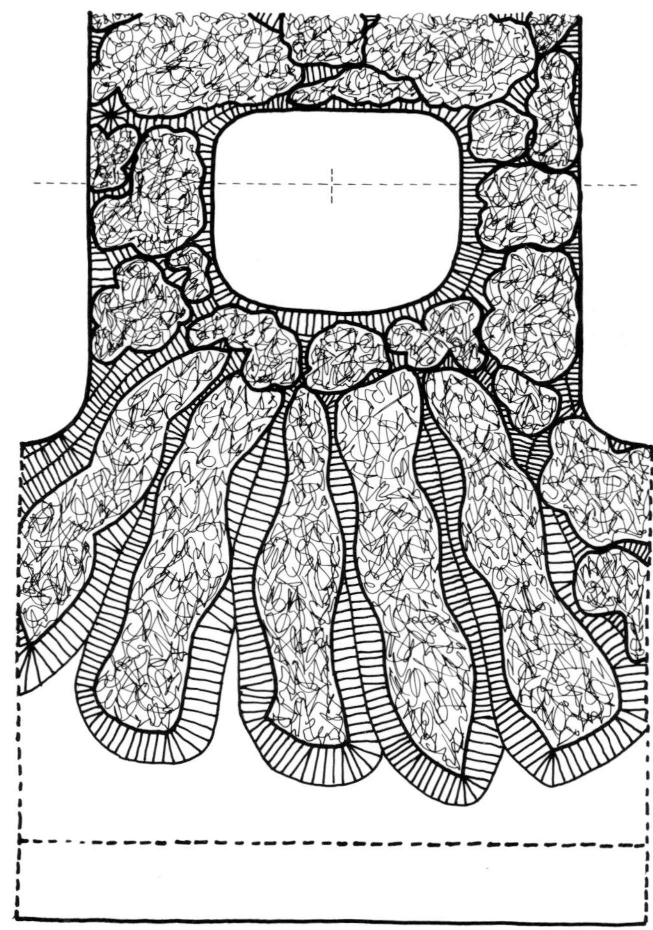

65b *. . . decide on the best arrangement, pin them to the template, and then fill in the spaces*

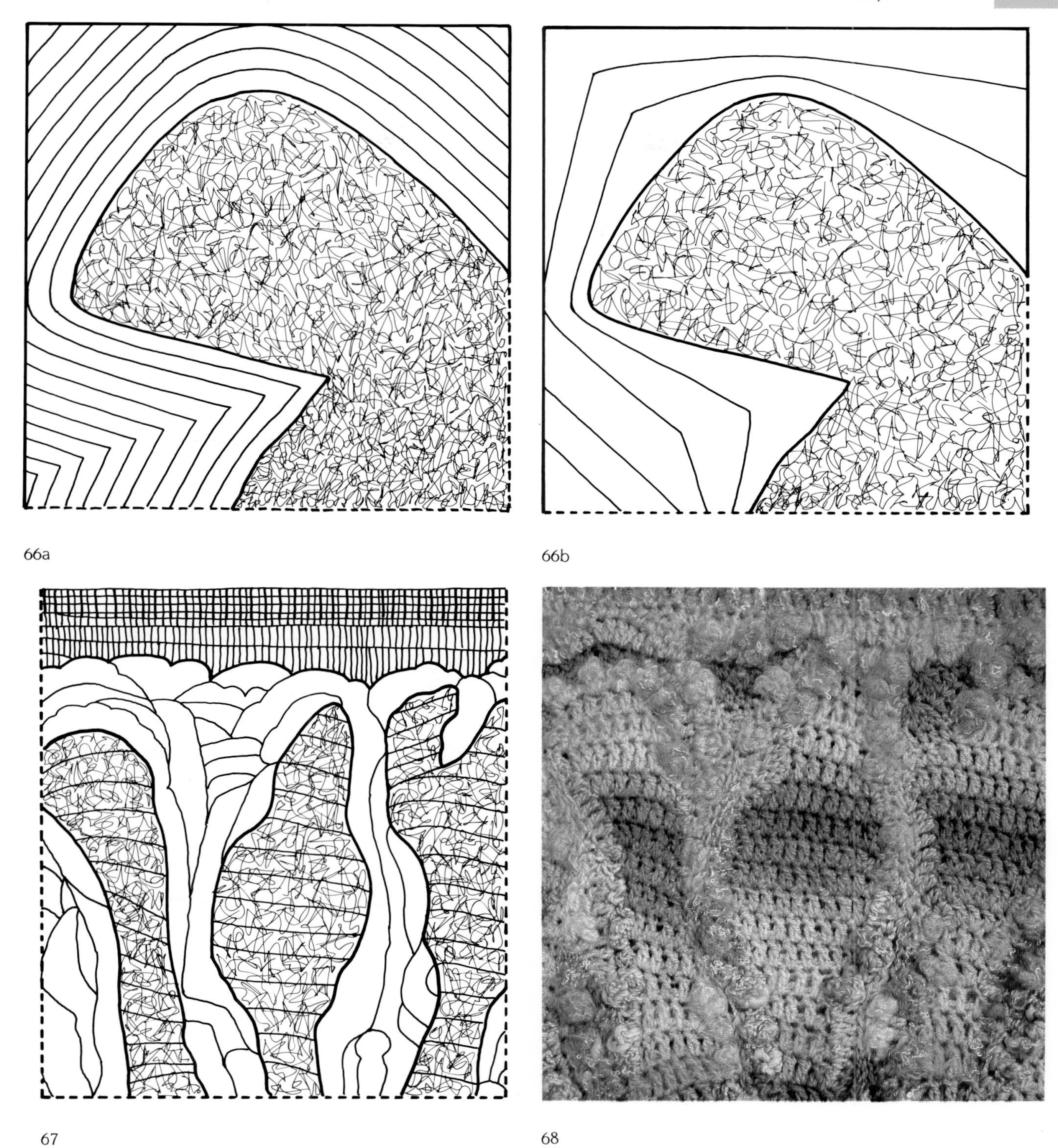

66a

66b

67

68

Patchwork

In conventional crochet patchwork means making squares, hexagons or other regular shapes in the same size and joining them together in regular formations. The Irish crochet lacemakers, however, made a great variety of different motifs, mostly based on flowers, leaves and sprays, then created a composition of these (which were sometimes breathtakingly complex and beautiful), basting them on to a drawing or template and joining them with an in-fill network to complete the fabric (69).

69a, b *Nineteenth-century Irish free-form crochet lace collar. The detail shows chain loops with picots forming the in-fill network and linking the individually made motifs*

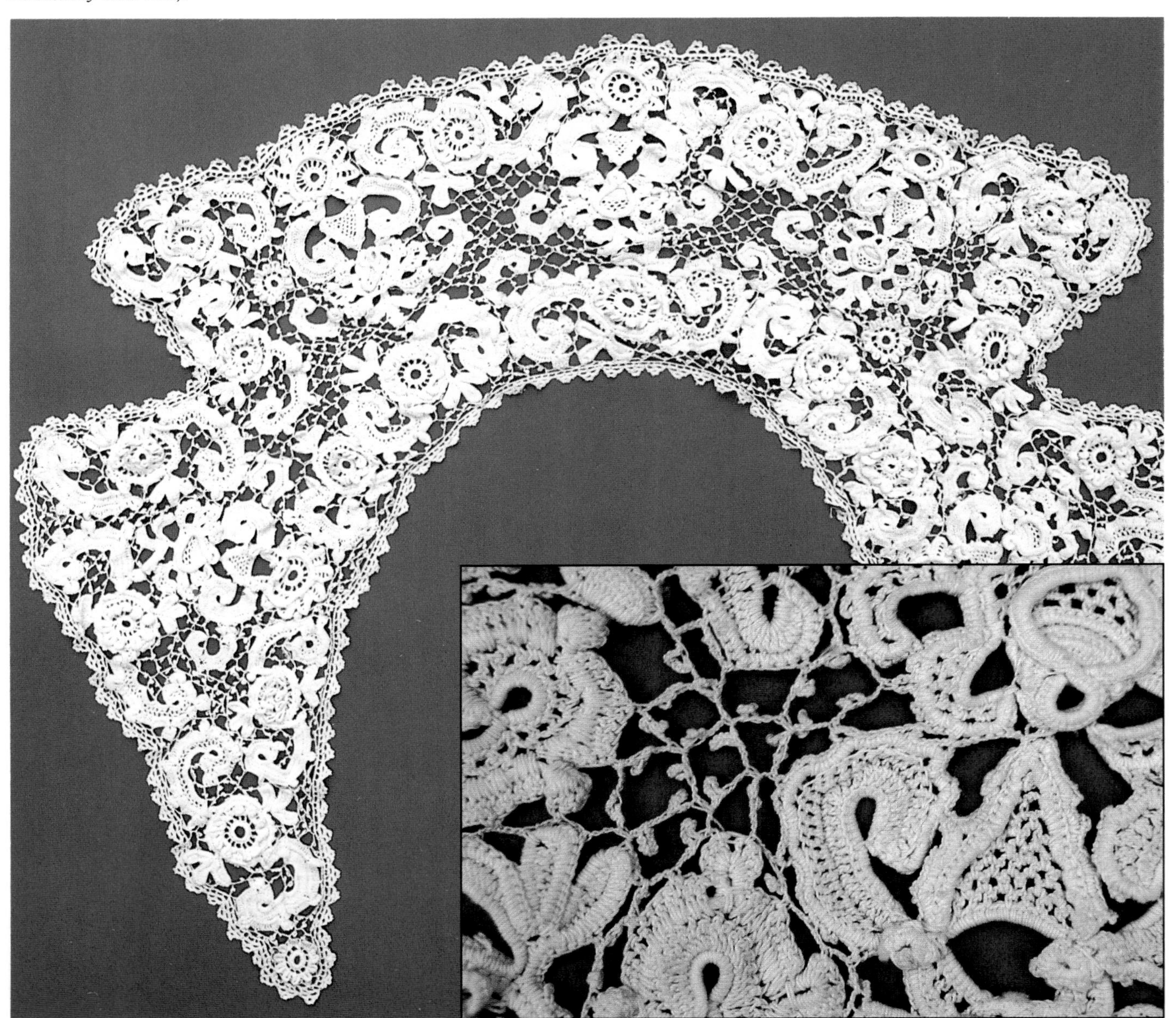

70 Free-form patchwork: random-shaped, textured 'scrumbles' assembled into continuous fabric for a cape

We have found that a most satisfying and exuberant way of making textured fabric is to make free-form crochet scrumbles of all shapes and sizes and join these, sometimes by sewing, sometimes with a crochet hook, either edge to edge or overlapping (70). There appear to be no useful 'rules' except to build lots of bobbles and assorted textured stitches into each stitch, always to make each piece different from the others, and to make sure that some are small, some larger, and some long and thin – irregular shapes fit together best.

Flat rounds, half rounds and cup shapes of different sizes can be joined together in an informal, organic way to resemble pebbles, fossils, bubbles, shells, sea urchins, lichen, etc. (71).

This way of working is easy to manage if the result does not have to be smooth or completely flat, because there is then scope to overlap and gather. If there is a need for all the pieces not only to lie flat, but also to fit accurately into each other, just arrange and pin them out on your template and look at the spaces between them: where they lie close, look to see how you could add to their edges to bridge the gaps. Where there are larger spaces, you can make new shapes separately to fit in, or, perhaps better, work directly around inside the space – starting, if necessary, with a chain 'bridge' to complete the circuit. Note that if you fill a space by working round and round inwards, it is difficult to work the final (centre) round, particularly if the fabric is solid. Instead, work clusters of three or four stitches, fasten off and finally join the centre neatly using a needle.

71 *A fossil-strewn, pebble beach*

72a, b *The organic 'growths' are made of surface raised stitches worked in clusters with the regular background stitches. They are not planned formally in advance, but are allowed to evolve spontaneously as you work*

73 At the edges of the textured area the bobbles are small and thinly spread; towards the centre they are thick, deep and crunchy. Variety is increased and enhanced by the fact that alternate rows are worked with opposite sides of the fabric facing. Once the textured area has been planned roughly, the exact arrangement of bobbles, etc., is best not charted, but left to spontaneous feeling

74a Parts of a formal diamond pattern (worked in surface raised stitches in clusters with the background stitches) have been left out in order to resemble a rock carving which has been worn away

74b When the multi-coloured yarn is white, simple basic stitches for background are worked. When each colour comes along, specific pattern elements are worked. The build-up of any pattern over several rows is therefore unpredictable in detail. (This approach can obviously be controlled by changing yarn colour deliberately, if you like)

Free-form colour and texture

Remember to think free-form when you are building up a raised surface effect or creating an area of texture, even when the background fabric is made of straight rows or regular rounds (72, 73).

Even the most formal and regular design can be transformed by some 'inverse' free-form thinking, when parts are made to crumble away spontaneously (74a), or to appear and reappear through the vagaries of colour (74b).

Whether you spin and/or dye your own yarns or find them ready-made, the most dynamic arrangements of colour and texture will flow from your hook if you are free enough to exploit the opportunities they offer. With multi-coloured yarns (75) one of the most beauiful and intriguing things to do is to make a simple fabric in short basic stitches, e.g. dc [US: sc], but to work a bobble or raised feature of some kind whenever the yarn changes to a particular colour (you decide which). The size of the bobble is selected and adjusted to use up exactly in one stitch or cluster all the yarn of the chosen colour there happens to be for the time being, and therefore to leave the other colours to form the 'background'. If the length of yarn in each colour and the sequence vary all the time, the result is an apparently random arrangement of bobbles in randomly graduated sizes – colourful, dynamic and exciting, and all without your having to make decisions about when or how big to make the bobbles!

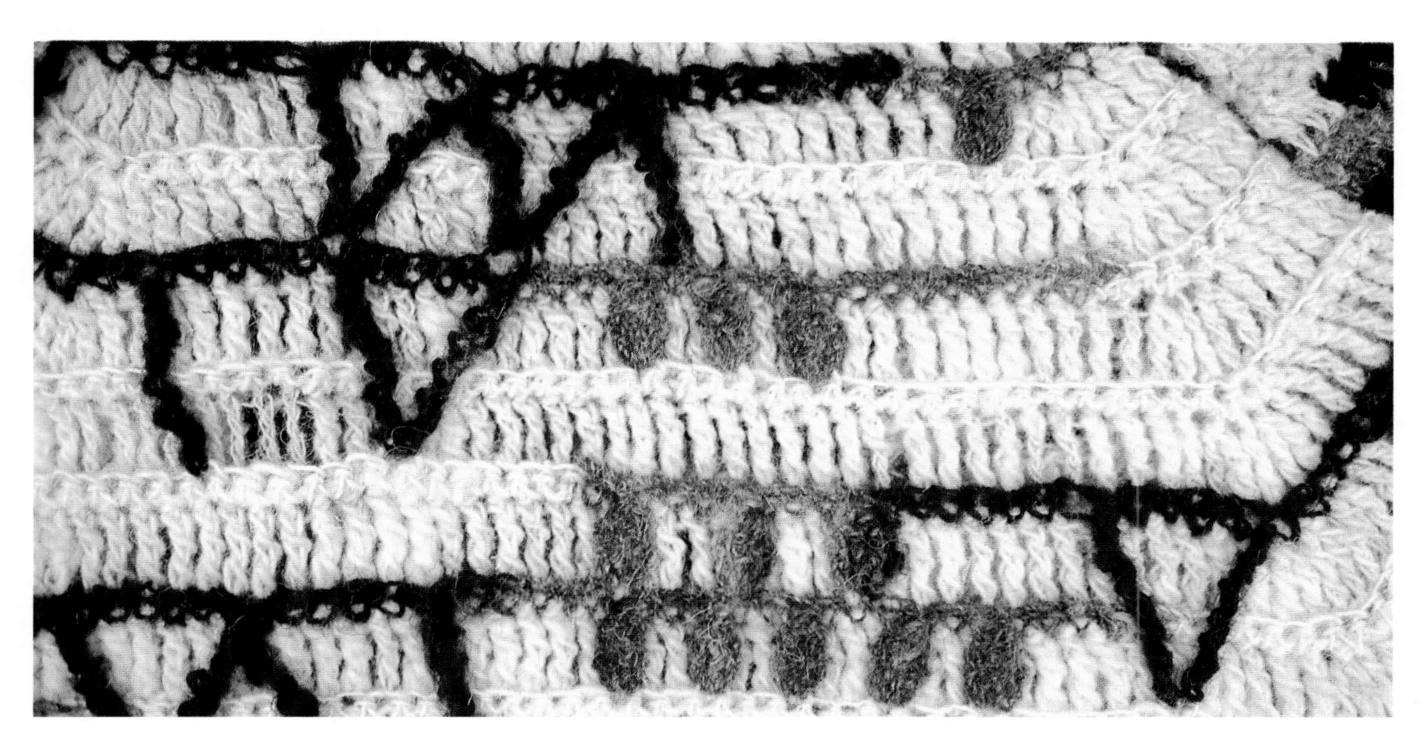

75 Multi-coloured yarn. There are four squares – both top ones and the bottom right are all made from the same yarn. The square at bottom left is made of a (different) yellow/red yarn: in its right half it has yellow bobbles on a red background, and these colours switch in its left half

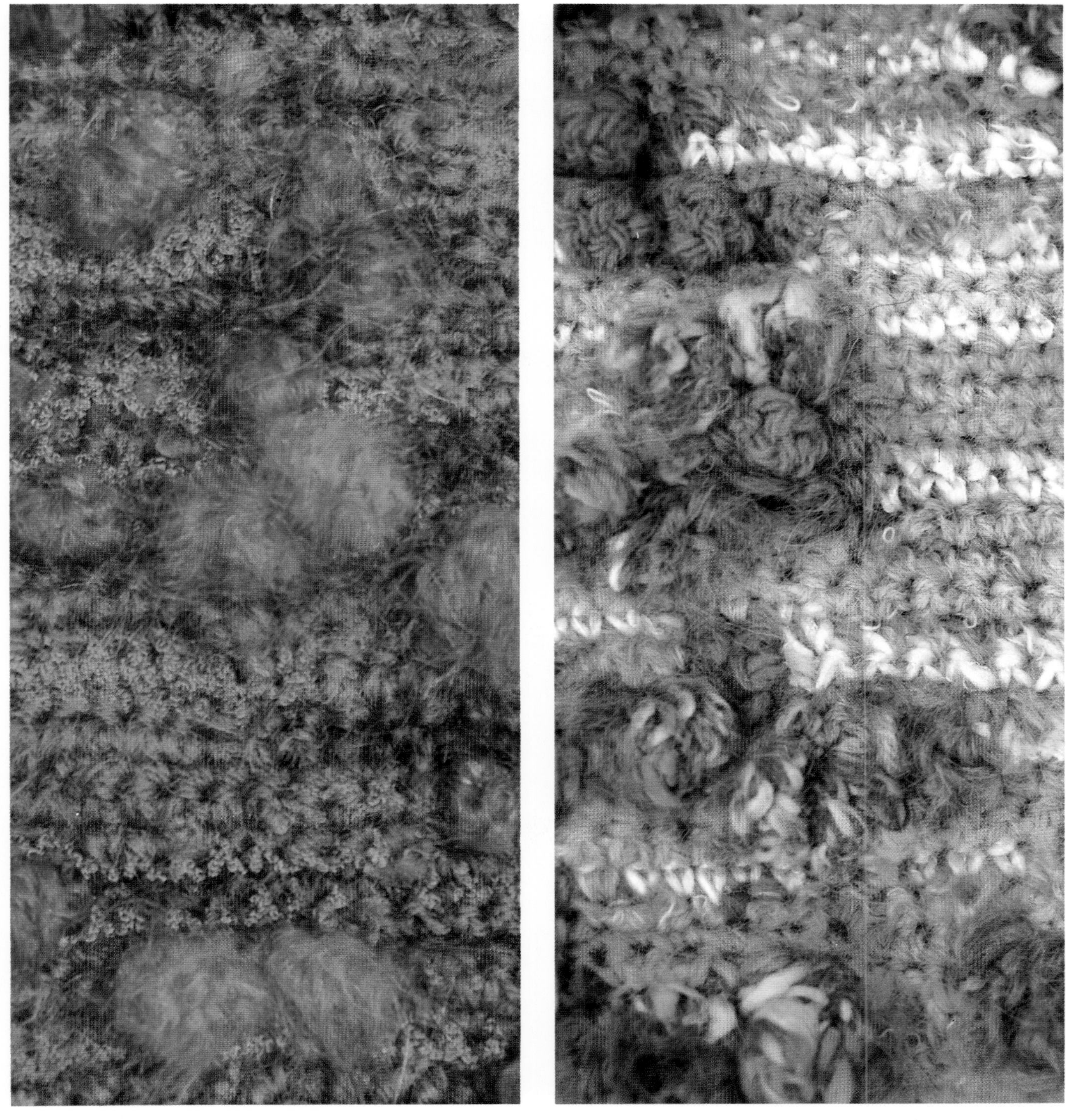

76a, b *Custom-built multi-coloured and multi-textured yarn*

Guidelines for random colour/texture work

Note that the measurements referred to here assume you are using a chunky [US: bulky] weight yarn with a 6.50mm [US: 9/10 or I/J] hook. For thinner yarn/hook combinations, scale the measurements down.

1. Choose a yarn with at least two predominant colours or colourways; use one of these for the bobbles.
2. With very short (i.e. less than 12cm [5in]) 'blips' or streaks of colour, make two or three chains and maybe slip stitch to the top of the previous stitch to form a picot which sits on the *right side* surface.
3. Make 'bobbles' as a single long stitch, 'bump', or cluster of long stitches joined together at the top roughly as follows:

Extent of colour	Bobble	
16cm [6in]	1tr	[1dc]
24cm [9½in]	1dtr	[1tr]
28cm [11in]	2tr	[2dc]
36cm [14in]	1dtr+1tr	[1tr+1dc]
40cm [15¾in]	3tr	[3dc]
42cm [16½in]	2dtr	[2tr]
48cm [19in]	1dtr+2tr	[1tr+2dc]
52cm [20½in]	4tr	[4dc]
54cm [21¼in]	2dtr+1tr	[2tr+1dc]
60cm [23½in]	3dtr	[3tr]
64cm [25in]	5tr	[5dc]
78cm [31in]	4dtr	[4tr]
96cm [38in]	5dtr	[5tr]

4. If you misjudge the length and there turns out to be insufficient yarn of the bobble colour to complete a cluster, pick up and draw through all the remaining loops prematurely, or re-make the last stitch as a shorter one.
5. If there is unexpectedly more yarn than you thought, add another stitch of suitable length (maybe only a short one) to the cluster before completing it.
6. Make sure bobbles always project on the right side of the fabric as you complete each one.
7. The programme in the yarn may happen to 'fit' the width of panel you are making and so the bobbles may come out in regular blocks or stripes. To disrupt this effect:
   a increase/decrease at one/both edges.
   b fasten off and rejoin each row, or make a few chains after turning to use up some yarn (fold these under afterwards when gluing your panel).
8. For variations, make other panels or patchwork squares with the same yarn, but swapping the colours used for background and bobbles – the effect is sometimes quite surprising.

Some yarns work better than others for these experiments, owing to the range of colours involved, length of yarn devoted to each, variety of the repeat sequence, etc. Hand-dyed yarns are particularly suitable.

Make your own, not only multi-coloured, but also *multi-textured*, balls of yarn by knotting together random short lengths of different yarns in carefully chosen colours (76).

Feel free to play these and other yarn and colour games: use several strands of fine yarn instead of a single thicker one (77). Change the thin strands in ones and twos to create more subtle colour effects.

77 *Fine yarns used in combination*

Three-dimensional shapes

There is no reason why your freedom should be restricted to two dimensions! Why not get involved in crochet sculpture (78, 79) and see where your imagination leads you? Exploit the elasticity of the fabric by stuffing with both soft filling and hard, rigid shapes; by twisting and by stretching.

Take a simple tube, for example: if you begin each round by increasing, but change to decreasing part of the way round, the tube forms a corkscew shape, which becomes wider or narrower depending upon whether you are gaining or losing stitches in the round overall (78a). What other amazing things can happen to tubes if, for instance, you also vary the stitch height?

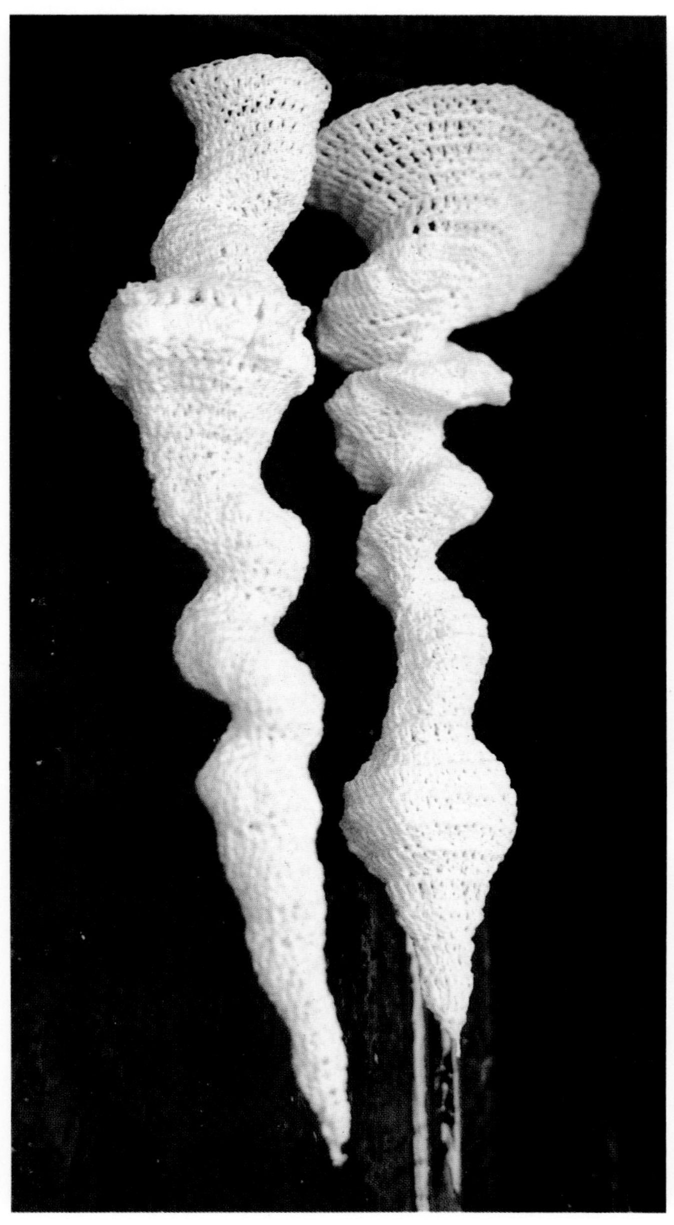

78a

78b

78c

78d

79 *Hanging chair: a simple cone shape kept rigid by a steel ring (which also frames the seat). You have only to sit in this chair for everyone to be convinced that you are in deep meditation and not to be disturbed – which can be most fortunate, when there are chores to be done! The hole beneath the seat was left so you could keep your yarn in the lower part – but you may find that the kitten takes it over*

4
Inspiration

People often imagine that 'inspiration' comes like a bolt from the blue, flying in at the windows of the imagination fully fledged and perfectly formed, needing only to be painted, written down, or crocheted as the case may be. In reality, ideas are far more often consciously and systematically mined. The raw materials have to be prised from the unyielding rock, refined with great difficulty, beaten into new shapes with great energy and then subjected to rigorous testing. Only a small proportion ever see the light of day again after their transformation.

The mining process may sometimes be a mental or spiritual one – an internal search down the corridors of the mind. Sometimes it may involve looking out at the world, seeing new things and finding familiar ones in new contexts. The important thing is always to be aware: once you begin to look, an abundant flow of ideas is guaranteed. The real problems lie more in remembering those fleeting ideas and in finding the time to develop even a small fraction of them. For most mortals it is essential to make notes, sketches and photographs and to collect specimens constantly. Then, when the daily shopping, cleaning, fetching and carrying, bread-winning, cooking and bottle-washing are all done, there will be something positive to get down to!

Just to get this notion of 'ideas' into perspective have a look (80) at our *Mind Map Key* for 'The Design Process' (this is a 'designer' expression meaning: 'What you have to think about and do when you are making something'). In order to answer the question in the centre ('What am I making?') everyone has to consider, consciously or not, all the factors featured around the ring. This is the kind of thing we mean by these:

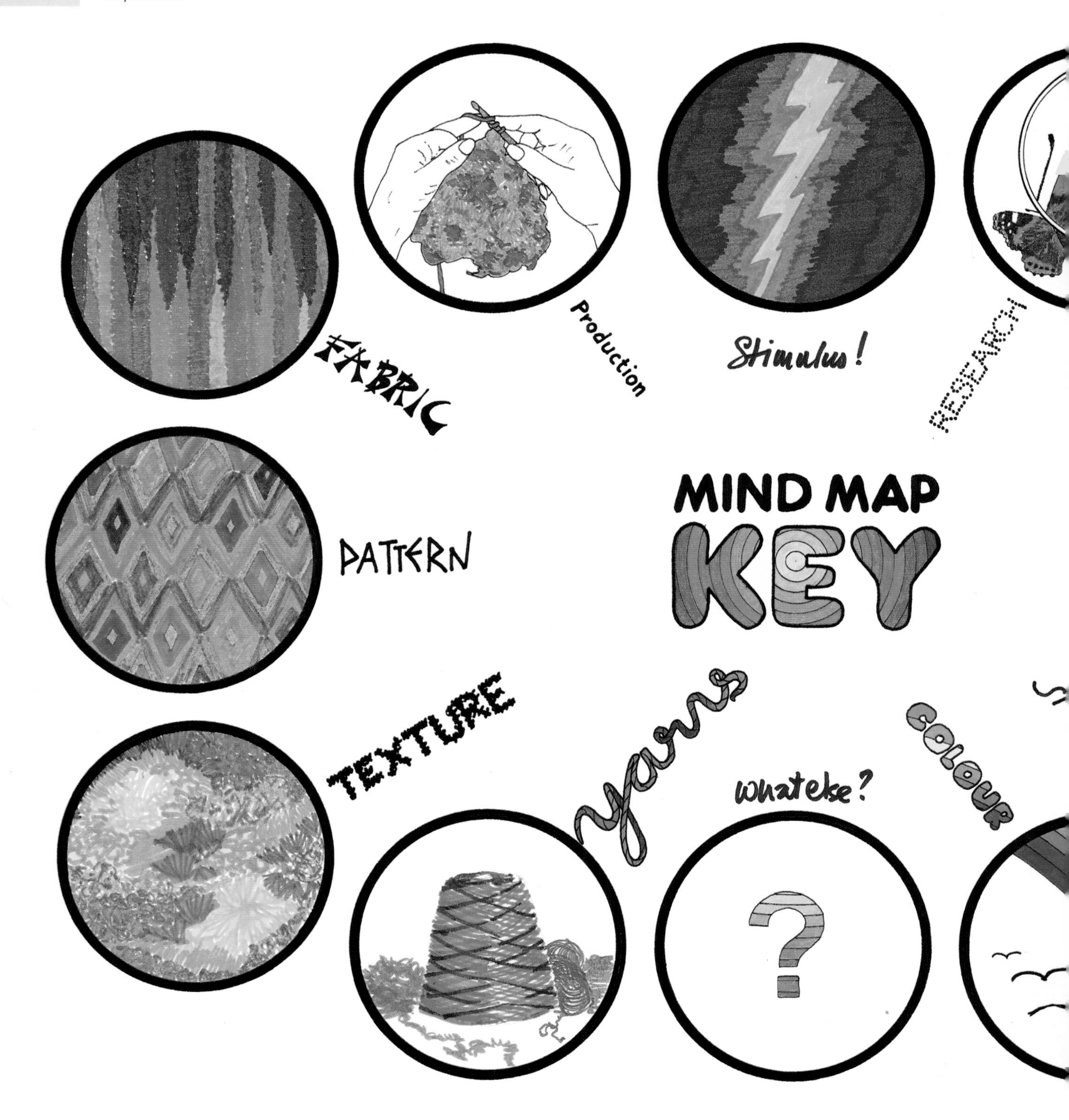
FABRIC
Production
Stimulus!
RESEARCH
MIND MAP
KEY
PATTERN
TEXTURE
yarns
whatelse?
COLOUR
?

Stimulus: this might be the sudden spark of a spontaneous idea or something emerging from everyday pressures – the realisation that it is someone's birthday next week, that rehearsals for the school play are coming up soon – or just the urge to get your hands on some crochet again!

Research: this covers all the things you do, regularly or in binges, to bring forward ideas for projects – looking, listening, making notes, etc. It may also include being on the lookout for people and/or places that might like your work (in itself another source of ideas).

Design: what is the overall design strategy? How is it affected by your talents and personality as a designer? You may enjoy a challenge and want to tackle a new and difficult design project, or to stick to familiar and comfortable procedures. Does graphing a picture give you nightmares, or is it what you insist on doing all the time? Does everything you make have to be practical or can you enjoy purely decorative and experimental work? Are you happy making trial swatches and good at arithmetic, or do you like to work intuitively?

Fabric: what sort of fabric does the project call for: light/heavy, thick/thin, solid/open, elastic/firm, smooth/textured?

Yarns: what qualities and characteristics of fibres and yarns would be suitable: thick/thin, smooth/slubbed/boucle/brushed, matt/sparkling?

Texture: what sort of texture needs to be achieved in the stitch work – smoothness/crunchiness/deep pile?

Shape and size: what are the implications of the shape and size of the whole project or parts of it: large/small, regular/irregular, geometric/organic, simple/intricate?

Pattern: does the project call for any special stitch patterns or arrangement of row construction?

Colour: does the project determine the colour range, or are you entirely free to create and play?

End use: who is it for? Where will it be hung/worn? (Think of the individual nature of the person and/or environment as well as the physical specifications.)

80 *Mind Map Key: the design process*

Production: how is it going to be made? How do you make thirty-seven crusaders' uniforms for that school play by next month with only two inexperienced crocheters to help you part-time? Whatever you imagined at the outset has got to be realistic in the end and suit the means of production!

Note that each factor is intimately and inextricably connected with all the others. Depending upon the project, the circumstances and your own personality, some of these factors will be more important than others at different times. Any one of them, however, may provide your stimulus or starting point! For example, someone's absolute priority may be a certain *colour*; you may have fallen in love with a newly discovered *stitch pattern*; a triangular window needs a fabric with a triangular *shape* – and most things need to be a precise *size*! If you have a passion for silky *texture*, you may never want to work with harsh twine; when you have just found a very exciting *yarn*, you will surely be looking for something to make with it.

Whatever your starting point, you will rarely get far before feedback from some of the other factors causes you to change tack and sometimes even nudges you into finding fresh creative solutions you would never have thought of from cold: you could never produce that sort of *fabric* with that *yarn* . . . that *pattern* is quite incompatible with that *shape* . . . you will never manage to *produce* that huge *fabric* on the bus to work, unless it is *designed* as a patchwork . . . so-and-so is allergic to that *yarn* fibre . . . The interplay between the different aspects of the design process itself sometimes generates more ideas than anything else!

Mind mapping your world

Think about all of this, then why not make your own *Mind Map Key* – one which represents how *you* really feel about the whole process? Can you think of any other factors? Or new headings which mean more to you than existing ones? When you are satisfied with your Key, take each factor in turn, write it in the middle of a fresh piece of paper and have a 'brainstorming' session, that is, put down everything that occurs to you under that heading. In this way you can make your own set of Mind maps (81) to include all the things that occur to you under each heading. (It is fun to do this in class or in a group, too, but you have to be able to write quickly!) These are the essential ground rules:

1. Do not try and make a neat, logical list, but put down all ideas and connections as fast as they come, in clusters and branches, wherever they seem to make most sense on the map.
2. It is vital to put down all thoughts – however scatty. Let them flow and wonder afterwards what they have taught you.

Notice how much overlap and interconnection there is. If you are ever short of an idea or get bogged down with a project in the future, the key will remind you how to make a new series of mind maps which will reveal a new generation of ideas.

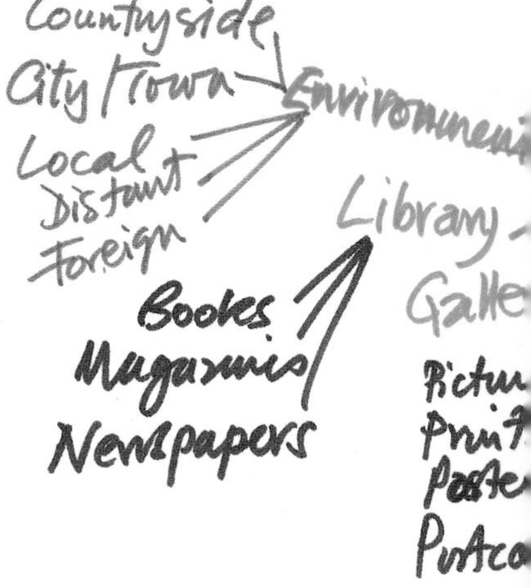

81 *Mind Map: stimulus*

Stimulus!

NATURAL
- Animal: Skin, Stripes, Fur, Scales, Feathers; Spiders' Webs, Butterflies, Moths
- Vegetable: Grass, Leaves, Trees, Bark, Fungi, Lichen, Fields, Hedges; Gardens, Water, Flowers — Cultivated, Wild, Dead/Dried
- Mineral: Stones, Pebbles, Fossils, Agate, Geodes
- Seasons, Weather, Sunsets, Clouds, Rainbows

Proportion
Colour - Texture
Form - Pattern
Feel - Shape

MANMADE
- Art: Painting, Photography, Sculpture; Monet, Klimt, Van Gogh
- Architecture: Roof-tiles, Walls, Tiles, Plasterwork, Hot air Balloons
- Ceramics: Jewellery
- Textiles: Weaving, Embroidery, Patchwork, Knitting; Hangings, Carpets, Kimonos, Screens

Supernatural
- Optical Illusion, Imaginary, Mirage, Dreams

IDEAS
- unconscious, conscious — mood, relaxed, sharp, receptive, sensitive, content
- Single, composite (putting ideas together)
- Useful, Practical, Beautiful, Exciting, Loving, Funny, Profitable
- Other, Crochet, etc — Historical, Traditional, Commercial Patterns, Magazines / Books, Stitch Dictionaries, Craft Guilds, Workshops; Home / Foreign

YARNS
- Colour, Texture, Feel, Fibre, Character, Quality

Chance
- "Bolt from the Blue", Objets trouvés

Research
- Listening, Seeing
- Notes, Sketch / Painting, Collecting
- Film / Photography: Colour, B&W; Wide-Angle, Telephoto, Soft-focus, Out-of-focus, Filters; Enlargement, Reduction, Distortion; Telescope, Microscope, Photocopier

82a

82b

Sources

We would like to share with you some of the things that regularly inspire us and some of our approaches to research. We hope that you will not simply want to copy our preoccupations and techniques (although you are quite free to do so), but will be inspired to develop and extend your own awareness and discover your own fresh pastures.

Our thoughts have been filled with the sky, landscapes filled with hills, fields, water, trees and hedgerows, beaches and gardens, walls, roofs and old carved stones encrusted with mosses and lichens (82, 83, 84). What will *your* imagination be working upon?

Landscape teaches us that there are millions more hues, tints and shades than you would think at first glance, and that shape, pattern and surface texture in Nature are never repeated absolutely.

Where we live the sky is constantly changing in colour and texture. We enjoy fluffy, cumulus clouds just before a storm, rolling around the sky, leaving patches of delicate blue between. We are always thrilled to see rainbows: what better starting point could there be for learning about how colour works?

Trees of all shapes and sizes can be represented in several different ways in crochet: as free-standing three-dimensional constructions (particularly inside wooden or metal rings) or as appliqué, surface crochet, etc. Notice how they change in all lights and seasons. In winter they make stark networks, which burst into green and then mixed blossoms in the spring, followed by infinitely rich and varied summer green, and autumn gold colours and textures. For texture, study their roots and trunks close to.

Just look, too, at the infinitely variable colours, textures and forms of distant fields, grasses and hedgerow plants. Hedges themselves are fascinating; often they are made of many different species melded harmoniously together.

Some things in Nature seem more crochetable than others. Although science has it that 'Robin's Pincushions' are the work of a gall-wasp, we like to believe that the hapless creature actually crochets them out of brushed mohair, and that things like dandelion clocks, thistledown and 'Old Man's Beard' are produced in a similar manner by some undiscovered species of spider in the dead of night!

We find the shapes, colours and textures of fungi irresistible – particularly certain kinds of bracket fungus with their semi-circular, fluted growths. Go looking for them in the countryside and also amaze yourself with the hundreds of varieties you will find in books.

The beach is a specialised kind of landscape which has never failed to fascinate us since early childhood with its sand, pebbles, shells, rockpools, fossils, and the forever-changing sights and sounds of the sea.

We love our countryside in all its forms and at all times

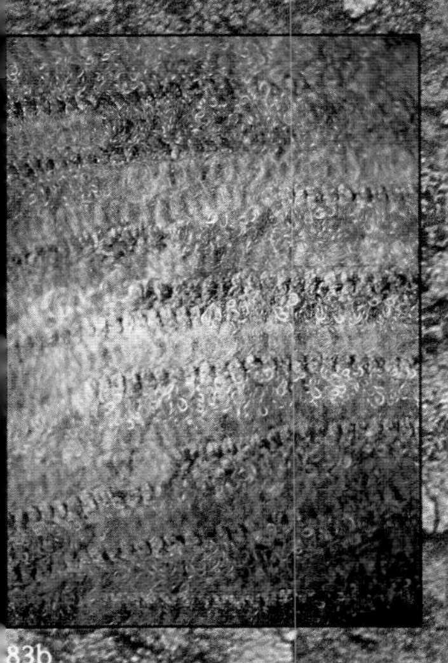
83b

83c

83f

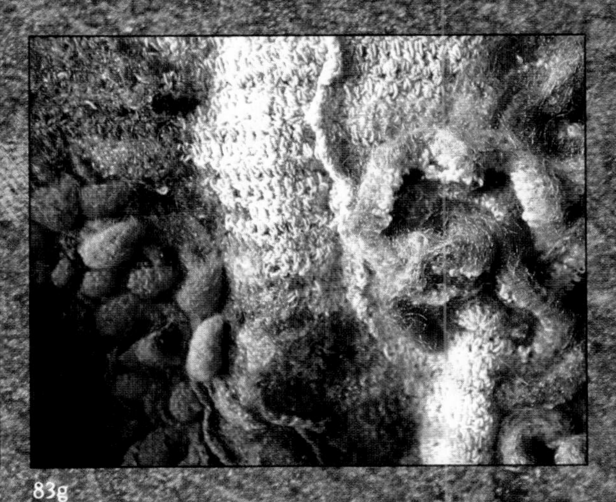
83g

83h

83i

and seasons, but 'landscape' also means where *you* are, or want to be – and that might include being out on the street or up in a satelite. It is hard to find a roof or brick wall in either town or country which is completely boring. Historically, lace patterns have echoed architectural features, particularly in the Mediterranean countries. There can be infinite variety in the colouring and patterning of your surroundings anywhere, even before mosses and lichens have gained a foothold.

Gardens of all kinds are intriguing in that they, too, combine the influence of man with the forces of natural growth. The painter Monet spent the last half of his life preoccupied with the riot of colour and texture his own garden provided at all times of the day and seasons of the year. We share his addiction and, as with landscapes in general, we cannot resist the bird's-eye view.

Butterflies and moths have always fascinated both of us. Apart from their myriad patterns, colours and textures, their shapes seem to beg to be made up into capes and ponchos! It has been said:

The butterfly,
even when pursued,
never appears in a hurry.

84a
84c
84g
84f

Research

We have found it essential not only to observe, but also actually to play with texture and colour as much as possible. At some time in your life, if only for a short while, we urge you to get to grips with handspinning and hand-dying.

Look hard and often at your surroundings. Make notes and try to sketch, draw and paint as often as you can. These activities are not just for artists, they are vital ways of making sure that we really are seeing what our eyes flick over.

How wonderful it is when you fold paper over on to fresh blobs of inks or paints, making colourful 'squidges'! This can now be serious fun – experiment with different colours and shapes and use the results as starting points for your crochet designs.

Cameras, telescopes, binoculars and microscopes remind us that there are different viewpoints from which to consider the same objects and different perspectives to be obtained. We began by using photography as a means of visual note-taking, but quickly we found it provided us with new images which were simply not apparent to the naked eye. A lens with a huge focal length and narrow field of view picks out hitherto unnoticed distant detail and puts it into surprising contexts. A wide-angle lens seems to spread the whole world at your feet. The ability to focus selectively picks out marvellous misty fore- or backgrounds which the brain normally does its best to hide from our consciousness.

Close-up lenses show us yet another secret world of pattern, shape, colour and texture. Infra-red filmstock, filters and accidents of processing reveal completely new colour rendering and balances. We are especially in love with the out-of-focus effects of catadioptric (mirror) lenses, which give a magical impression of brushed mohair crochet texture through their soft, intermingling doughnut-shapes.

If you never look, you will not find; if you *do* look, you will need to be very strong-willed indeed not to forget all about what you were looking for in the first place amidst the profusion of fascinating new things you had never even dreamed about, yet which continually rush in and out of your viewfinder (85)!

85a

85b

85c

85d

85e

85f

85g

5
Getting it together

We have already discovered that getting down to it – translating ideas into practical projects – can easily be a roundabout process. Some ideas will come to you slowly and remain on the back burner for years, whilst others will flash into your mind and demand to be taken up and completed in a single white-hot burst of energy. Others will seize your imagination and your time in surges. If you are working to commission or for some particular occasion, deadlines will loom and you will *have* to get on, like it or not! The chances are that you will always have several projects at different stages of development on the go at once; there will always be more ideas queuing up and shouting to be started than you can ever hope to get around to, because apparently there will never be enough time . . . all this is normal!

Yarns

When you have some project ideas in mind, be energetic but patient in the very important search for (and/or preparation of) the right yarns – you are going to need many more than you think. If you are starting from scratch or have not yet built up a rich stock of yarns for yourself, you may have a great deal of exciting foraging to do. You can usually start to crochet before you have acquired everything (you may well have no idea how much you are going to need anyway), but it is wise to have gathered together enough to represent the overall character of the project (86).

Colour is likely to be very important and it will help to have some colour reference (maybe scraps of yarn, but also see 'Inspiration 1' below) and carry this around with you in case you have the opportunity to look for yarns. For your search you will also need to have some idea of what general thicknesses, textures and qualities are going to be appropriate and will work with each other. What practical considerations are there? Are fibre content and durability as important as appearance and feel? Here are some things to think about.

Structure and feel: warm, soft, slippery, springy, light, fragile, elastic, cold, hard, tough, heavy, hard-wearing, smooth, crepe, velvety (chenille), hairy (brushed), lumpy (slub, knop), loopy and crinkly (bouclé)

Visual: dark, rich, pale, pastel, matched tones, contrasting, hot, cold, matt, shiny, glittering, translucent, luminescent, sparkling, plain monochrome hues, striped (mixed ply), heather mixture, fleck, marl, space-dyed, spot-printed, multi-colour

Fibres: alpaca, angora, cashmere, cotton, flax (linen), llama, mohair, silk, sisal, wool; acrylic, lurex, metallic, nylon, polyester, viscose

You may already realise that there could be a great deal to learn about yarns if you want to become really familiar with their qualities and characteristics and be able to match them with the requirements of your projects. Take one step at a time, because this is a long-term voyage of discovery. Here are some guidelines:

1. Go for what interests you first and concentrate on those things; let other aspects make themselves known to you in their own time.
2. To begin with, stick to one general thickness of yarn in a given fabric (this includes using two or more thinner yarns together to make up the same general thickness).
   To get a better idea of the thickness which fancy and slub yarns really will work up to, fold them into four strands, twist them up and compare with a smooth yarn treated in the same way. Generally these yarns are best treated as though they were as thick as their thickest parts.
3. If you are not yet confident about handling colour, it is wise to choose to restrict your palette in one of the following ways:

   Monochrome: use as wide a range of tones as you like, including dark shades and light tints, but keep to the same basic hue (87a).

   Analagous: whatever range of tones you use, stick to colours which are adjacent on the colour 'wheel', which runs from red through orange, yellow, green, blue, violet and back to red (87b).

   Monotone: whatever range of colours you include, make sure they are all of a similar tonal value or strength (87c).

   Inspiration 1: find any object (pebble, shell, leaf, picture postcard, magazine illustration, a paint 'squidge' of your own, etc.) which appeals to you purely for its colours. Look at this very closely and find yarns to match *all* the colours you can find in it; notice how these go together and in what proportions they appear (87d). Have fun learning!

   Inspiration 2: find a multicoloured yarn you like and then find plain coloured yarns in a variety of textures and qualities to match each of its colours (87e).
4. Think about hand-spinning and/or dyeing your own yarns. Try vegetable and mineral dyes as well as synthetics, dyeing in the fleece and dip-dyeing in the hank, ball or cone. (Dyeing your own may still be the only way to obtain all the colours and tones you want across a wide range of different textures.) Try working with exotic materials as cheap and cheerful as old cut-up tights, rags and plastic bags, or rubber bands, plastic tube, string, wire (88) and rope.

86 *Yarns: mixed colours and textures. You will probably need many more than these for a project, but this could be a nucleus. Notice the different textures and qualities as well as the colours*

87a Monochrome

87b Analagous

87c Monotone? Which ones would you leave out to ensure an even tone?

87e Yarns selected to match the multicoloured cone in the centre

87d Yarns selected to match the rock in the centre

88 Exotic Yarns! Fusewire is surprisingly easy to work with – particularly if you work Solomon's knots – and you can thread small beads on it, without the use of a needle, quicker than on to any other 'yarn'

Stitch and fabric

What yarns look and feel like in the hank or in the ball is one thing; what they can become when you crochet with them may well be another. Experiment as much as possible with all kinds of yarns; try different solid and openwork, smooth and textured stitch patterns and different sizes of hook to find out how they work out in your hands. Notice particularly how things like weight, density, elasticity and drape change: crochet can be made as frail and wispy as gossamer, or solid and rigid enough to stand on its own without further stiffening (89). If you are really meticulous, you may remember not only to keep all your trial swatches, but to tag them with a reminder of what yarn they were made of and what size hook you used.

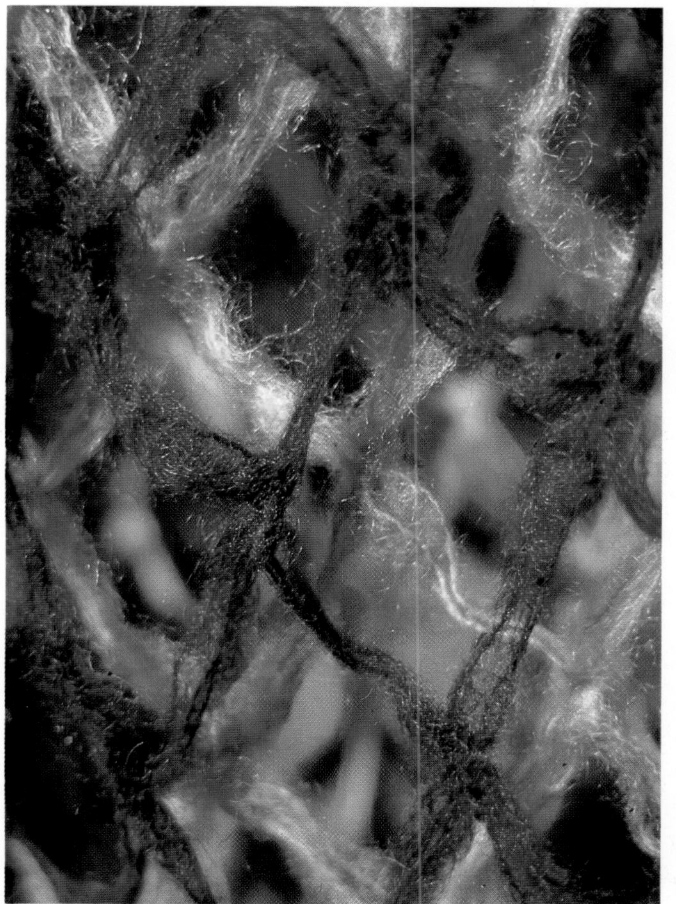

89 Openwork Solomon's knots in brushed mohair have a hazy effect – particularly when the double thickness fabric moves . . .

Construction

If you want to make conventional garments, such as sweaters, you need to study existing examples, noting how the different pieces for front, back and sleeves are shaped and fit together (90). Compare the overall look and style of the garment as worn with the subtle details of the shaping (if any) of the individual parts; notice where and by how much bigger they are than the figure they are designed to fit. Again, follow your own inclinations: if you enjoy making only thick, generous, baggy sweaters, do so and let someone else design skinny and finely shaped ones – or vice versa.

Seams

Even when making garments in more or less conventional rows, we prefer to eliminate the usual seams as far as possible – especially those which occur at the sides of the fabric pieces. We join tubes (sleeves and sweater bodies) as we go and often make sleeves and bodies continuous. Depending upon the direction of working, we may have a single seam either across the top of the shoulders and sleeves or down the centre (back and/or front). These seams run in the same direction as the rows of stitches and so it is easy to work a row of slip stitches through both thicknesses at once with the right sides together, matching stitch for stitch (93).

Remember that, instead of making two separate pieces of fabric and joining them afterwards, you can work twice into the same base chain – that is, once in the normal way and then again into what was the underside – so that the fabric grows away from the base chain in opposite directions. This enables you to work from the middle of a garment towards the edges or, more commonly, to add welts and cuffs (90).

When you want to take the business of designing further, to try different shapes, for instance, experiment with the positions of seams, etc. It is often useful to make up dummy garments out of cheap material first (these may often serve as templates, too – see below). That way you make your mistakes and solve your problems in advance.

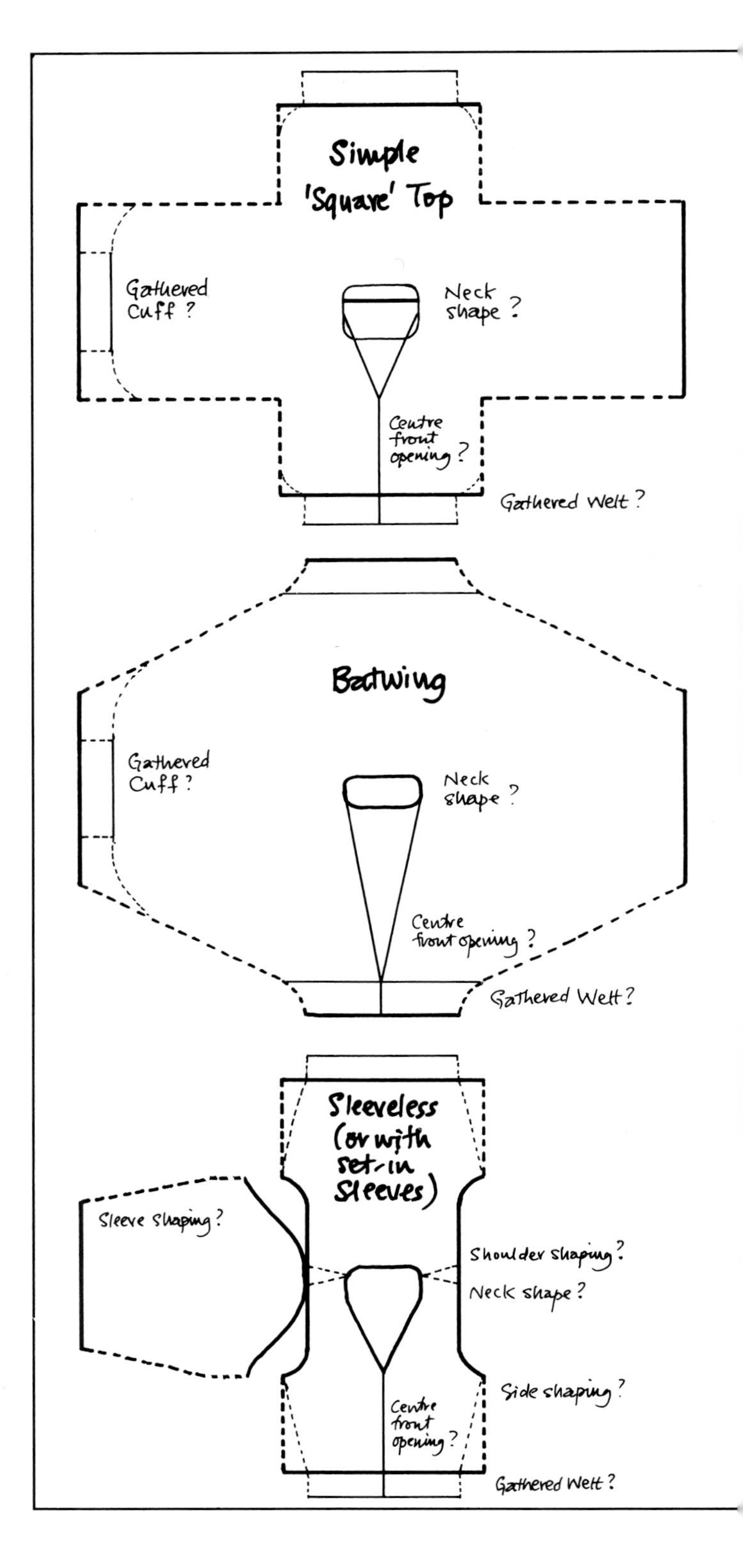

90 Basic garment shapes and working plans. Although it may be convenient for the purpose of sketching, designing and planning to separate a garment into pieces, you can still usually make the fabric continuous and so eliminate seams – even when you are working to a regular row structure

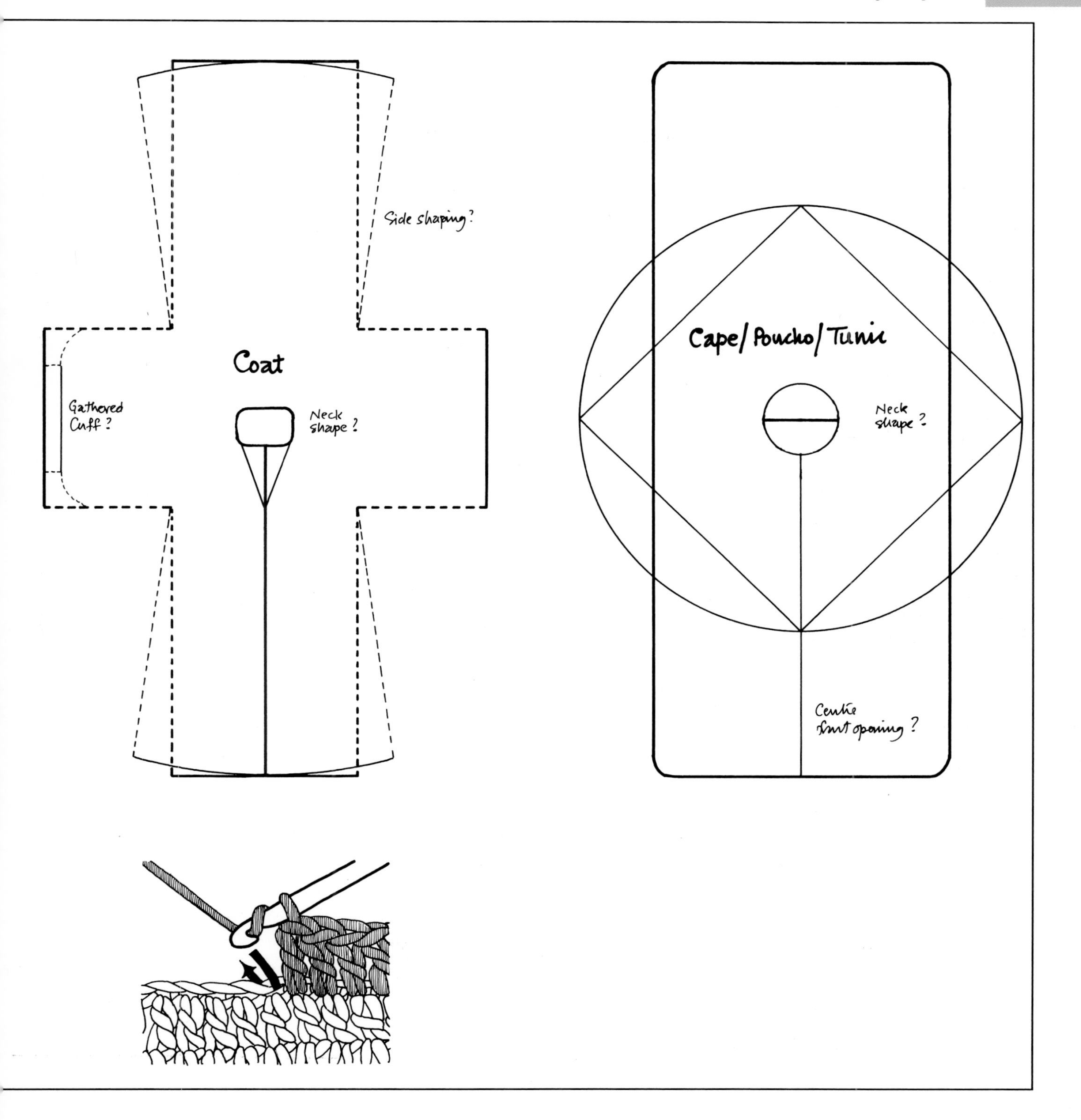
Side shaping?
Coat
Gathered
Cuff?
Neck
shape?
Cape/Poncho/Tunic
Neck
shape?
Centre
front opening?

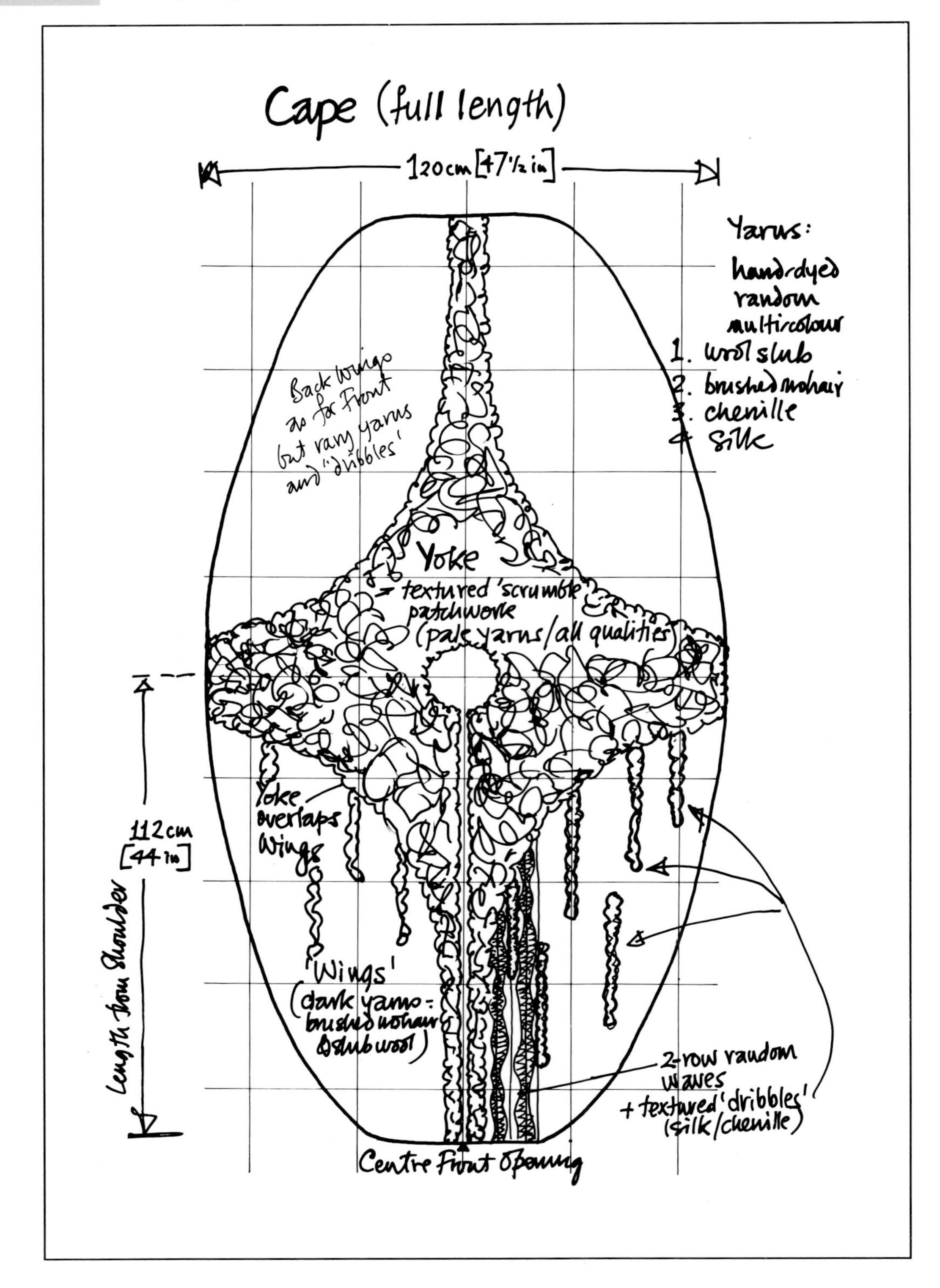

92 Full-length cape

91 *Working sketch for the template of the cape*

Templates

For free-form crochet, particularly when making garments, we work to an outline shape. For several reasons this is best drawn on to a flexible but stable (woven) fabric, such as an old sheet or blanket, which is easy to draw on accurately and can stand having lots of small pieces of fabric pinned and re-pinned to it. (Otherwise wrapping paper or wallpaper will do, as long as it is big enough.) Usually a template can be cut out roughly, tacked together, slipped on and checked for fit. It can then be modified, if necessary, before you are committed to the crocheted fabric.

Drawing

We usually rough out our ideas in thumbnail sketch form first (91, 94), then draw the full-size template, putting in only as much detail of the design as we find useful. To draw large shapes accurately, it helps to draw a regular squared grid on to the template first. To make sure symmetrical shapes match exactly, we draw one side only, fold the template down the middle, pin through both thicknesses along the lines to be reproduced, turn over and draw in the matching lines as indicated by the pins.

Starting the crochet

Where you start the actual crochet depends not only upon the specific project, but on your own skill and how you feel! You may start tentatively on what you think may be the easiest or least important parts and slowly gain confidence. Or you may not be able to resist plunging in at the deep end and going for the most exciting and demanding aspects, breaking new ground. You can expect your expertise, moods and appetites to change and be reflected in the ways you handle your crochet.

We usually insist on hedging our bets and keeping our options open. This includes making designs which will not tyrannize us from the moment we start to crochet, but which can be adapted and modified as the work progresses. Sometimes, when the work turns out not to fit any lines we happen to have drawn on the template, if we nevertheless like what we have done, we may choose to re-draw the lines rather than re-make the work!

A large template for a large project may be inconvenient to take around with you. Instead it may be possible to make a separate tracing of a section you want to work on away from base on a manageable piece of paper.

Quilting

If you choose the right material for the template, you can quilt the crochet fabric down on to it, so that it becomes the permanent lining of your finished garment.

Joining

When you work in the way suggested, you need have no conventional seams as such, but there may still be a great deal of joining to be done. Sometimes you will use a crochet hook for this and at others you will sew with a wool needle. What you use and how you use it will depend upon two main things: your personal preference and what you are trying to achieve.

The needle joining techniques we use most are woven, overcast (whipped) and backstitch; otherwise we like to crochet edges together with slip stitch (93) on the wrong side. Double [US: single] crochet and longer stitches worked on the right side create a pronounced ridge, which can feature as an integral part of the design. When the main fabric is openwork, the joins may well need to be crocheted to complement the pattern.

Each of the possibilities has different characteristics, advantages and disadvantages and you will probably need all of them at some time or another. The more techniques you are aware of and can handle, the more likely you are to find the ideal solution in any circumstances.

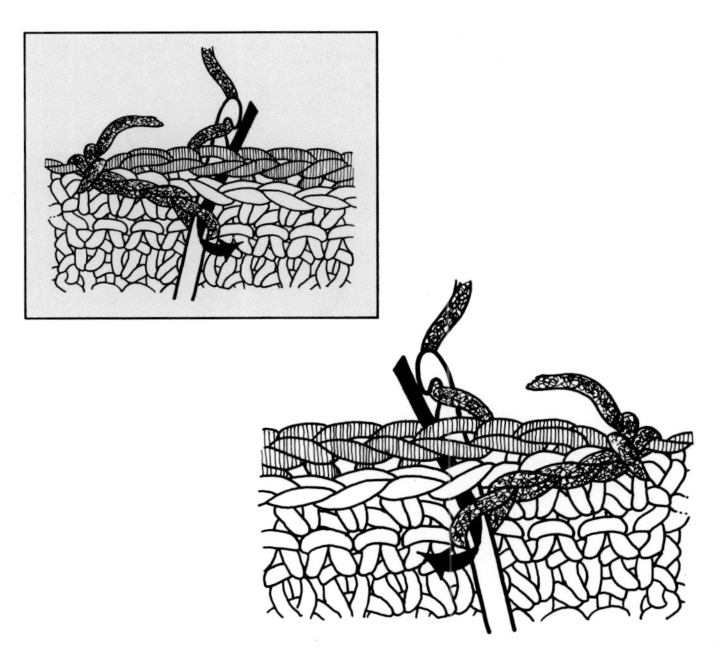

93 *Joining with crochet slip stitch*

Edgings, welts and cuffs

We generally find it most suitable to leave cuffs, welts, etc. until last. It is helpful to be able at the end to amend our original thoughts about length, stitch pattern, fullness and gather, and it is simple enough to work directly on to the edges of the otherwise made-up garment.

Some knitters, who are not entirely confident of their crochet, nevertheless like to finish their knitwear with crochet edgings. Many people who do make crochet garments, however, automatically finish them by hand, knitting the cuffs, welts and edgings. Our favourite method of making cuffs and welts is in crochet rib and we often like to complete straight edges of all kinds with corded (crab) stitch (95).

95 *Crochet* 1×1 *rib. Row* 1: *1RtrF, 1RtrB [US: 1RdcF, 1RdcB]; *rep from* *. *Row* 2, *etc*: RtrF *round each stitch now projecting at the front and* RtrB *round each stitch now projecting at back of the fabric as you currently view it. Notice also the corded (crab stitch) edge. Since crab stitch tends to be fuller than crochet rib, be prepared to miss a stitch every so often to achieve a neat effect*

94 *Working sketch for the template of the coat shown on pages 70–1*

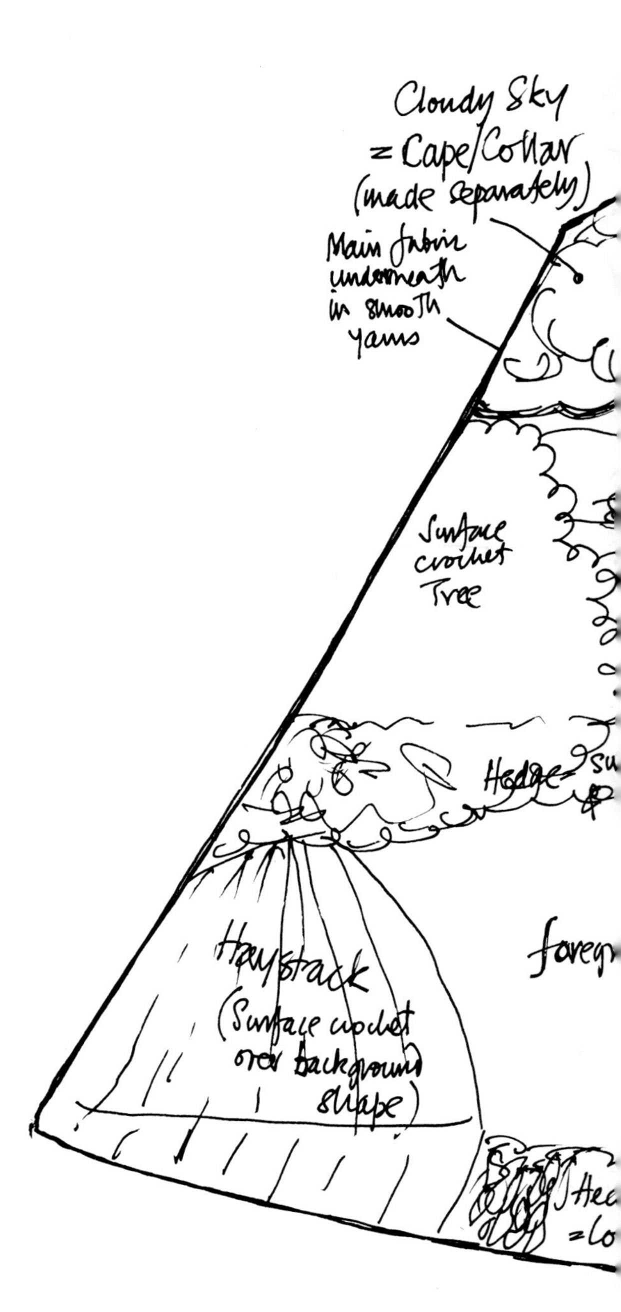

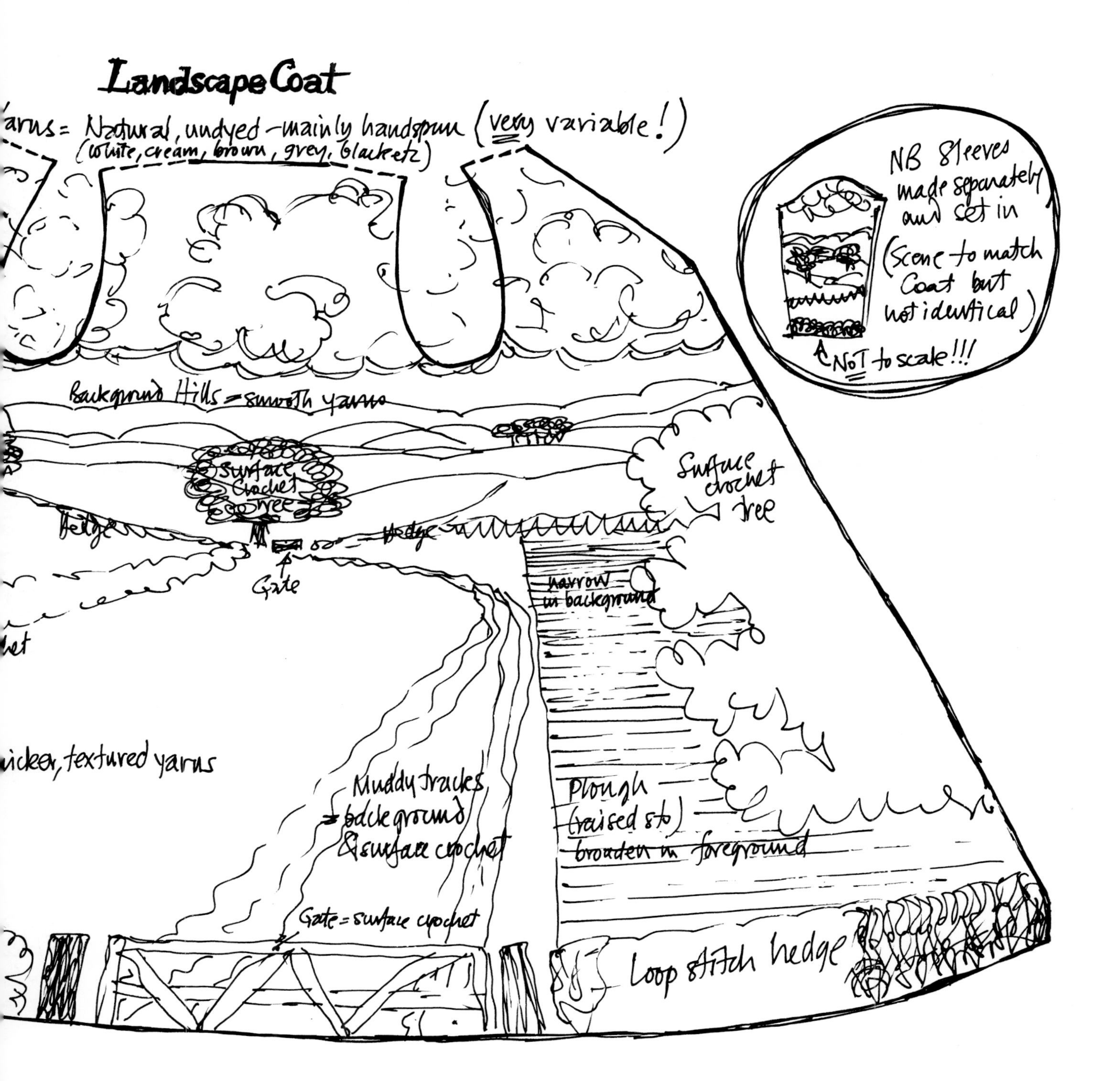
Landscape Coat
Yarns = Natural, undyed – mainly handspun (very variable!)
(white, cream, brown, grey, black etc)
NB Sleeves made separately and set in
(Scene to match Coat but not identical)
NOT to scale!!!
Background Hills = smooth yarns
Surface crochet tree
Surface crochet tree
Hedge
Hedge
Gate
Harrow in background
thicker, textured yarns
Muddy tracks background & surface crochet
Plough (raised sts) broaden in foreground
Gate = surface crochet
Loop stitch hedge

Rings, frames and panels

Rings, frames and simple panels are the formal means of presenting the results of our artistic endeavours. They give us special opportunities to experiment, because they allow us to get into making free-form creative fabric, which does not have to be wearable, nor fit a precise shape.

Rings

Although we use both wooden and plastic rings, most often the thin metal rings intended for lampshades and sometimes coated with plastic (96) are best. Despite their being intended for use as frames flat against a wall, rings are especially suitable for mobiles (remember to make both sides interesting and different). It is usually easiest to make the fabric separately and join it to the ring afterwards. Make sure the fabric is *smaller* than the ring, so that you have to stretch it to fit. Then crochet or sew the edge of the fabric to the ring.

When rings are used as a framework for trees, it is more suitable to work directly on to them; they enable you to construct a flexible skeleton of trunk and branches and then add the foliage directly, keeping the tree shape fluid (97).

Frames (98a, b)

Make sure the fabric is *larger* than the cut-out in the mask. In the case of thick fabrics, you may need to pack the space between the mask and the backing to avoid buckling.

96a

96b

Small wood Panels (98c)

Make sure the fabric is larger than the panel, so that the edges can be wrapped around the back and stapled or glued; any irregular edges are then hidden (99). Wood panels make it easy to pad or stuff the fabric for enhanced three-dimensional effects.

Large Panels (100)

We tend to attach the crochet fabric to a hessian panel and lap this around a simple timber frame in the same way as the small panels.

General reflections

Common sense and an open mind are our best friends. We try to keep our thinking free, so that we can see and respond to the direction our work seems to be taking. Then we can change our minds and make modifications with the least amount of disruption, unravelling and reworking. But to make things work effectively or to achieve what we are really after, we sometimes *do* have to pull out and start again – more than once. From time to time we may be totally baffled and frustrated, and even lose confidence. All that seems to be quite normal, too!

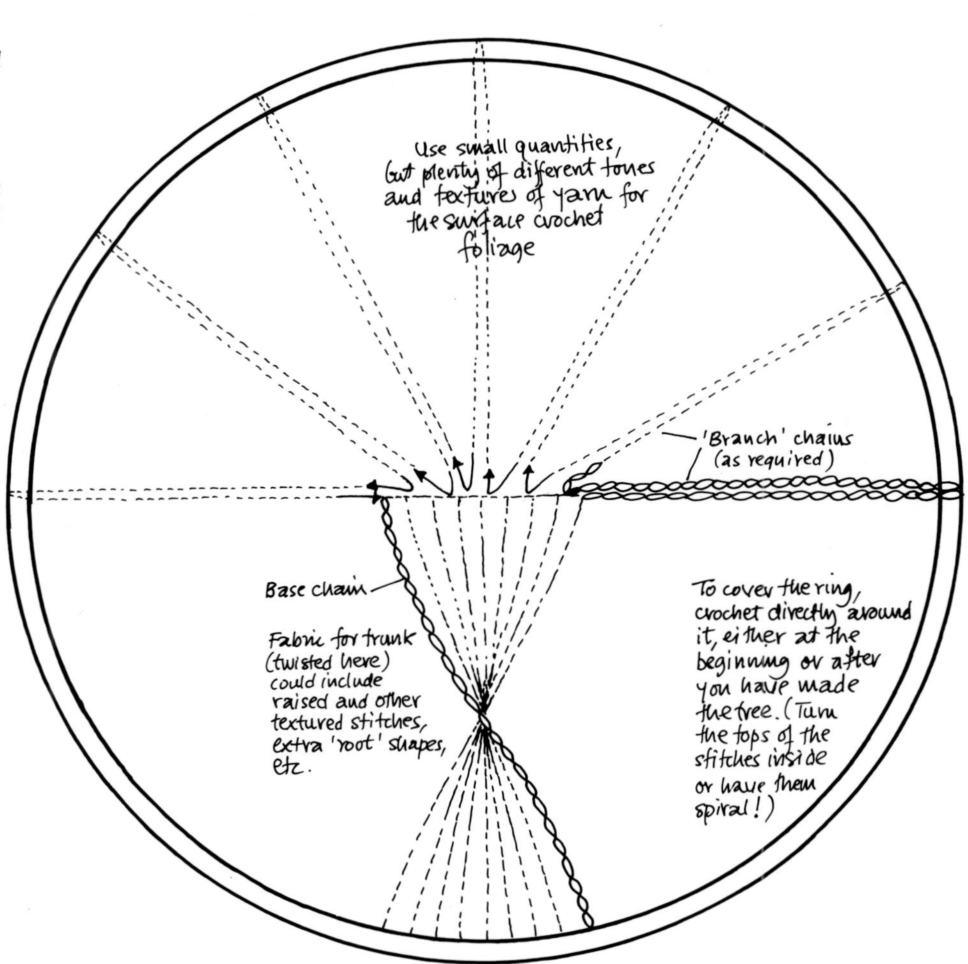

97 *Tree ring construction: the trunk is made first and attached by crochet or sewing to the ring at the roots.*
A simple framework of branches is made by chaining out to the ring, anchoring with a slip stitch and chaining back again several times.
The foliage of chains, Solomon's knots or other stitches can then be added with surface crochet

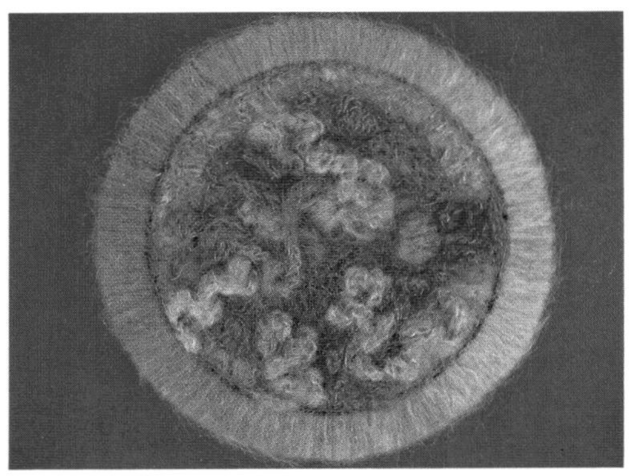

98a This 'ring' is really a circular cut-out card 'frame'. The 'picture' behind it is mounted on the solid card disc cut from its centre. The ring is wrapped with the same yarn that was used in the centre.

98b A roughly shaped piece of fabric can easily be framed . . .

98c *. . . or folded around a wood panel and stapled*

99

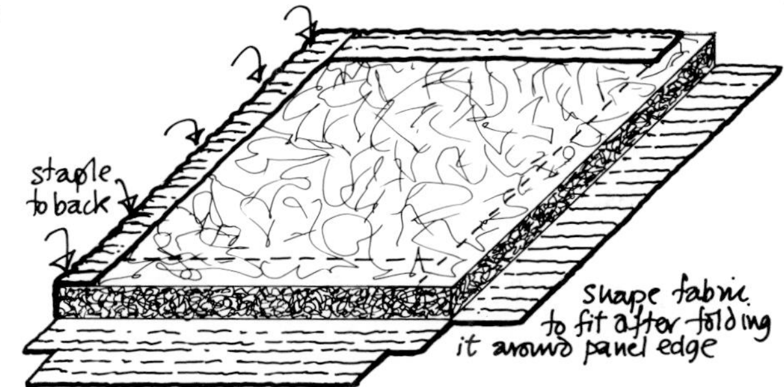
staple to back
shape fabric to fit after folding it around panel edge

100

Useful information

Basic terms/abbreviations/symbols

UK	Abbreviation	International symbol	US equivalent	Abbreviation
stitch(es)	st(s)		stitch(es)	st(s)
chain(s)	ch(s)	○	chain(s)	ch(s)
space(s)	sp(s)		space(s)	sp(s)
double chain	dch		single crochet chain	sch
treble chain	trch		double crochet chain	dcch
turning chain	tch		turning chain	tch
starting chain	stch		starting chain	stch
slip stitch or single crochet	ss or sc	•	slip stitch	ss
double crochet	dc	+	single crochet	sc
half treble	htr	T	half double	hdc
treble (yrh ×1)	tr		double crochet	dc
double treble (yrh ×2)	dtr		treble	tr
triple treble (yrh ×3)	ttr		double treble	dtr
quadruple treble (yrh ×4)	qdtr		triple treble	ttr
quintuple treble (yrh ×5)	qntr		quadruple treble	qdtr

yarn weights

UK	US
4 ply	fingering
double knitting	sportweight
aran	knitting worsted
chunky	bulky

Hook sizes

International Standard Range (ISR) (Figs = diameter of hook in mm)	US equivalents Wool		Cotton
10.00			
9.00	15		
	13		
8.00	12		
	11		
7.00	10½	K	
6.50	10	J	
6.00	9	I	
5.50	8	H	
5.00	7		
4.50	6	G	
4.00	5	F	
3.50	4	E	
	3	D	
3.00	2	C	
			0
2.50	1	B	1
	0		2
			3
2.00			4
			5
1.75			6
1.50			7
			8
1·25			9
			10
1.00			11
			12
0.75			13
0.60			14

Useful addresses

Guilds, etc. – for details and how to join:

The Knitting and Crochet Guild
Mrs Elizabeth Gillett
Membership Secretary
5 Roman Mount
Roundhay
Leeds LS8 2DP

The Association of Guilds of
Weavers, Spinners and Dyers
The Secretary
BCM 963
London WC1N 3XX

The Textile Society
Barbara Ingram
Membership Secretary
19 Ty Mynydd Close
Radyr
Cardiff CF4 8AS

For resources for teachers and parents, including books and booklets, teaching packs, projects leaflets, wallcharts, slide sets, videos and audio-visual learning programmes, workshop courses, etc:

The Knitting Craft Group of the
British Hand Knitting
Association
PO Box 6
Thirsk
North Yorkshire
YO7 1TA

For everything to do with crochet:
The Crochet Design Centre
17 Poulton Square
Morecombe
Lancashire
LA4 5PZ

Specialist Suppliers:

Colinette Yarns
Park Lane House
7 High Street
Welshpool
Powys
Multi-coloured, hand dyed yarns; patterns, workshops, etc. (Mail order)

Texere Yarns
College Mill
Barkerend Road
Bradford
West Yorkshire
BD3 9AQ
Enormous range of all kinds of yarns, also budget assortments (Mail order)

William Hall & Co
(Monsall) Ltd.
177 Stanley Road
Cheadle Hulme
Cheadle
Cheshire SK8 6RF
Wide range of plain and textured yarns, especially undyed (Mail order)

Rowan Yarns
Green Lane Mill
Holmfirth
West Yorkshire
Extensive and reliable range of plain colours (ask for your nearest stockist)

Lodge Enterprises
56a Ayres Street
London SE1 1EU
Filoni yarns (Mail order).

Crochet collections:

Gawthorpe Hall
Burnley
Lancashire

The Victoria and Albert
Museum
Cromwell Road
South Kensington
London SW7

Textile Study Centre
"Windover"
Wynniatts Way
Abberley
Worcestershire
WR6 6BZ

Index